A Guide to
Managing a Profitable Business

Finance without Fear

William S. Hettinger, Ph.D.
John Dolan-Heitlinger, MBA

THE INSTITUTE FOR FINANCE AND ENTREPRENEURSHIP
WINDHAM CENTER, CONNECTICUT

Published by The Institute for Finance and Entrepreneurship, LLC
Windham Center, CT 06280 USA
(860) 456-4477
www.financewithoutfear.com

Book design by TLC Graphics, *www.TLCGraphics.com*
Cover: Monica Thomas, Interior: Erin Stark

The publisher greatly acknowledges all of those who reviewed copies of the manuscript and covers throughout the creation process. Your input was invaluable.

Library of Congress Cataloging-in-Publication Data

Hettinger, William, 1955 –
Finance Without Fear: A Guide to Creating and Managing a Profitable
Business / William S. Hettinger, John Dolan-Heitlinger

   p. cm.
Includes index
ISBN-10: 0-9828917-0-4
ISBN-13: 978-0-9828917-0-4
1. Finance. 2. Financial statements. 3. Business enterprises – Finance.
4. Corporations – Finance.
I. Hettinger, William S., 1955 – II. Dolan-Heitlinger, John, 1952 – III. Institute
for Finance and Entrepreneurship (firm) IV. Title

Proudly printed in the United States of America

Bill dedicates this book to his wife Ann-Marie.
Thanks for being there as I worked on this book.
Your input is more valuable than you will ever know.

John dedicates this book to his wife, Eileen.
You are the best thing that ever happened to me.
You make me want to be a better man.

Table of Contents

Detailed Contents

Chapter 4

Chapter 5

Chapter 6

Chapter 7

Part 3: Tools to Help You Make Money

Chapter 11

Working Capital and Operational Efficiency 159

Part 4: Building and Operating Your Business to Make Money

Financial Empowerment

 To many people, the world of finance is mysterious and intimidating. The simple mention of a profit and loss statement, balance sheet, or cash flow projection creates anxiety and a churning in the stomach.

Many people are simply not comfortable with finance and prefer to avoid it. While it may be possible to avoid finance in your personal life, or perhaps defer it to a spouse, this isn't always possible or advisable in the world of business. It is very important that small-business owners and managers understand finance since it is the root of how businesses make money.

An owner or manager who understands finance has a leg up on the competition. If you understand finance, you have the ability to analyze the structure and operations of your business and use this information to structure the company in a way that will allow the business to pay its bills, earn a profit, and maximize its financial performance.

Financial results are one of the prime scorecards by which businesses are measured. For anyone who's involved in owning or managing a business, some knowledge of its financial operations is necessary so that correct decisions can be made about its growth and operations. This knowledge is also important so the owner or manager can understand the information prepared by the accountants and finance department.

The purpose of this book is to remove the fear of finance for entrepreneurs, small-business owners and managers. We believe that one of the reasons finance is too often viewed as something that is mysterious and complex is simply the way the material is presented. Finance books are too often written in accountant-speak and contain formula after formula to calculate anything and everything but ultimately explain nothing.

Traditional finance books are built starting with accounting and explain how transactions are booked, how they affect the balance sheet, and then how to bring these transactions forward into balance sheets and profit and loss statements.

Other finance books are written to help investors analyze a business from an investment perspective (should I invest in the business or the stock?). They typically include an explanation of financial statements and how to use ratios when analyzing a company for investment.

Finance Without Fear focuses on explaining how to understand the financial statements of a new or existing business, as well as how to use financial tools to maximize the value of the business. If you understand finance, you have the knowledge and power to create an effective and profitable business.

Who Should Read This Book

Finance Without Fear is a guide to finance for entrepreneurs, business owners, managers and board members. The book is intended to be a key resource on using financial tools to create value in a business.

The book has three main purposes:

1. To explain financial statements

2. To explain how to develop financial projections for businesses using financial statements and financial analysis tools

3. To explain how financial statements and financial statement analysis tools can be used to help a business make money

Readers of this book will most likely be interested in developing a working knowledge of finance and financial tools that can help them build and grow a business. This book is ideal for:

1. Entrepreneurs starting or growing a business

2. Managers seeking to apply financial management techniques to their business

3. Board members who need to understand the financial aspects of the business

4. Graduate and undergraduate students in management and entrepreneurial business programs

This book is not intended to be an all-encompassing financial management text but rather a guide that will explain the key elements of finance and how to use finance as a tool.

There is also a companion workbook to *Finance Without Fear,* the *Finance Without Fear Business Forecasting Workbook,* that will guide you through the development of financial projections for your business.

Structure of the Book

Finance Without Fear includes the traditional material explaining the various components of the cash flow statement, profit and loss statement and the balance sheet. This core knowledge helps the entrepreneur, business owner and manager manage a business. Beyond this core knowledge, the book will explain how financial statements and financial analysis tools can be used to help a business make money.

The structure of the book will first present the theory—the basics of finance and competitive advantage—and then apply it to the process of creating and forecasting financial statements for a business.

Finance Without Fear incorporates a series of case studies of various types of small businesses. Many existing financial-statement-analysis books focus on manufacturing companies that use traditional measurements, such as inventory and cost of goods sold. But in today's economy, many businesses aren't manufacturers but rather small professional service organizations, service businesses, and retail establishments.

The case studies in the book include a professional service organization, a retail operation and a manufacturing business. The case studies and examples emphasize the unique characteristics and financial statements of each of these types of businesses. For instance, rather than cost of goods sold, the profit and loss statements may include items such as cost of services provided, the business may have no inventory, or the accounting might be on a cash basis.

The book blends theory with these case studies and uses those examples to demonstrate how to develop and forecast financial statements for a particular type of business, as well as how to analyze a specific business within the context of other similar businesses.

Finance Without Fear is divided into four parts:

1. Part 1 (Chapters 1 to 2) introduces strategies used by businesses to make money and will introduce the sample companies we'll use as examples throughout the text.

2. Part 2 (Chapters 3 to 9) explains the content and meaning of the basic financial statements.

3. Part 3 (Chapters 10 to 15) explains how to evaluate the information on financial statements and how this information can be used to help a business make money.

4. Part 4 (Chapter 16 to 21) discusses how to build and operate a business to make money, as well as focusing on taxes, accounting, and how to find the money to start and operate your business.

We hope by the time you've finished this book the world of finance will be less mysterious and intimidating, and you'll feel empowered to take control of your business's finances.

Part One

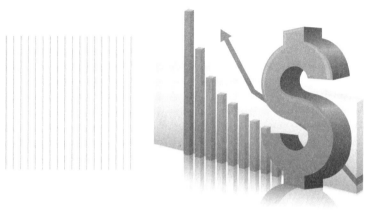

Introduction

Although at times it seems that finance is a world unto itself, the truth is that understanding finance is one of the keys to operating a successful and profitable business. Finance and financial decisions are an integral part of the operations and operating strategies of a business. A business owner or manager who understands finance has at his or her fingertips a wealth of information about the business that can be used in many ways to help the business make money.

In the first part of this book, we introduce the key types of operating strategies that businesses use to create a competitive advantage in the marketplace. We also introduce three typical companies—a manufacturing company, a retailer, and a service business—that we'll use as our examples throughout the book. These operating strategies and sample companies will be integrated into our discussions as we explain financial concepts and demonstrate the use of financial tools.

CHAPTER ONE

How Businesses Make Money

Anyone who has ever visited New York City probably remembers his or her first visit to Fifth Avenue. Fifth Avenue has always been one of the premier shopping streets in the world. The sidewalks bustle with shoppers. There's a constant flow of traffic in the street. The store windows are decked out with the latest fashions and electronic equipment. Clearly, Fifth Avenue is a retailer's dream. If you have a store on Fifth Avenue, you've "made it."

But let's look at Fifth Avenue more closely. If you've been to Fifth Avenue more than once, you've probably noticed that some of the stores are different each time you visit. Last year's fashion store has been replaced by a newer, trendier fashion store. The shoe store has become an electronics store. The travel agency is vacant. The restaurant has new owners and a new name. Even the world-famous Scribner's bookstore is now a cosmetics store.

Perhaps Fifth Avenue isn't a dream for all retailers. Some businesses have had their store on the street for decades and have been very successful. Many others have opened and closed in the same time frame.

Even if you've never been to New York, you've probably taken this walk in your own community. You may have walked up and down Main Street or through the shopping mall. During your walk you probably saw something similar to Fifth Avenue. Some businesses are full of customers and still located where they've always been. In other places, a new business has replaced the one you remember. In still other places, the business you remember is gone and the store sits empty.

Clearly, there's a difference between businesses. Some have been successful and continue to thrive, while others haven't been as successful and continue to struggle, and still others have gone out of business completely.

If you own a business or are thinking of starting one, you'll want your business to be successful. For your business to be successful, your business will need to make money. It's that simple.

Let's begin by taking a look at the strategies a business can use to help it make money.

Key Business Strategies

A business makes money by selling goods and services to customers for more than it costs to provide those goods and services. Those businesses on Fifth Avenue that have survived for many years have learned how to do this. Those businesses that failed weren't able to figure this out.

The businesses that have survived have a competitive advantage over those that haven't. Competitive advantage exists when a business is able to continually to sell its products or services for more than its competitors or is able provide its products and services at a lower cost than its competitors[1].

There are four key strategies that a business can use to compete and differentiate itself from the competition:

---

[1] The concepts of competitive advantage and the value chain were introduced by Michael Porter in his book *Competitive Advantage: Creating and Sustaining Superior Performance*.

1. Innovation and design
2. Operations
3. Sales and marketing
4. Customer service

For a business to survive and prosper over the long term, it must have a competitive advantage. To achieve a competitive advantage, the business must have expertise in at least one of these areas. A business can be average, or even below average in the other areas, but it must have expertise in one of these four areas.

If you're starting a business, or currently own one, it's important to understand your areas of expertise and how they can be used to help your business make money.

To effectively sustain and grow your business, you'll need to recognize your expertise and apply it to building a competitive advantage for your business.

Innovation and Design

One strategy businesses can use to compete in the marketplace is to offer unique and innovative products and services. Unique products and services are in some way different from the products and services offered by the competition.

Let's look at some examples of innovative and unique products and services:

- A consulting business might employ highly skilled and specialized individuals who provide consulting on client projects.

- A research company might use proprietary models to analyze data or have collected substantial amounts of data not available elsewhere.

- A restaurant may employ a famous chef able to prepare specialized dishes that allow the restaurant to offer a dining experience available nowhere else.

- A clothing company might partner with a famous designer to design seasonal clothing lines.

- An electronics manufacturer may have designed a unique video game that keeps users involved for hours at a time.
- An artist may create a series of unique and highly sought-after paintings or sculptures.
- A pharmaceutical company may have a patent on a drug that it has spent years developing and testing.

A business that offers unique and innovative products and services is often able to charge a higher price for those products and services. Customers are willing to pay more for unique and innovative products that they feel provide increased value or satisfaction. The higher price paid by the customers translates into greater profits for the business.

Operations

The second strategy that a business can use to compete in the marketplace is operations. Operations refers to the operating processes of the business. In a manufacturing business, operations includes the process of taking in raw materials, converting them to finished products, delivering the products to customers, and receiving payment from those customers. In a retail business, operations includes the process of receiving products, making the products available to customers, and selling the products to customers. For a service business, operations includes receiving requests for services from customers, providing services to customers, and receiving payment for those services.

A business that operates efficiently will be more profitable than a business that is operated inefficiently. Let's look at some examples:

- A manufacturer can automate a manual production step, improving quality and speeding up the production process.
- A manufacturer can switch to a just-in-time inventory process, reducing the amount of money the business has invested in inventory.

- A retailer can link its cash registers and inventory management systems so merchandise is automatically reordered as it is sold.

- A service business can implement time management and reporting software to simplify its billing and improve its collections process.

If a business operates efficiently, it will be able to produce and sell products at a lower cost than its competitors or provide services at a lower cost than its competitors. By reducing its costs, the business makes more money.

Saving money in operations is an ongoing strategy for many businesses. The operations of the business need to be continually reviewed, looking for opportunities to improve efficiency and save money. A business that does not focus on the efficiency of its operations may find itself falling behind, unable to compete with more efficient businesses.

Sales and Marketing

Sales and marketing is the third strategy a business can use to compete in the marketplace. Sales and marketing refers to the process the business uses to make customers aware of its products and to build desire for its products.

The goal of a sales and marketing strategy is to make customers aware of your products and services and to differentiate your products and services from those of your competitors.

There are many examples of businesses that have used sales and marketing as a strategy to make money:

- Many consumer companies have spent millions in advertising to build consumer awareness of their businesses and their brand. The consumer recognizes the name and is willing to pay more for it.

- Pharmaceutical companies use a dedicated sales force to market their products to medical professionals.

- Food-service companies stock the shelves in supermarkets so their products are placed where a customer is most likely to see and purchase their goods.
- Internet-based companies spend marketing dollars advertising on search engines to attract customers looking for a particular keyword or topic.

Customers buy products or services from a business because they provide some benefit or satisfy some want or need. That is, the product or service provides value to the customer.

When used effectively, a sales and marketing strategy can make a product (or brand) known to potential customers and perceived to be of higher value than competing products. When customers perceive the product to be of higher value, they are willing to pay more for the product, and the business can make more money as a result.

We started this chapter by saying Fifth Avenue is a premier shopping street. Fifth Avenue is exclusive. Fifth Avenue is a brand. Customers are willing to pay more to buy from stores on Fifth Avenue. Retailers are willing to pay more to locate their stores on Fifth Avenue.

Customer Service

The final strategy a business can use to compete and differentiate itself is customer service. Customer service is the activities that support the customer during and after the purchase process. These can include:

- A knowledgeable and helpful sales force
- An easy buying process
- Website, manuals and instructions that are easy to understand and use
- Customer service representatives who answer the phone and are knowledgeable and respond to customer needs

- The availability of parts and assistance in obtaining repairs
- The fulfillment of implicit and explicit commitments to the customer

A business that excels at customer service can build a strong relationship with the customer. When a strong relationship exists between customer and business, the customer is more likely to make additional purchases from the business, offer favorable reviews, and be a source of referrals.

A business that has strong relationships with its customers can leverage the relationship to obtain premium pricing for its products and make more money.

Where's Your Focus?

The business strategies outlined above focus on the two key elements of operating a business: providing a product or service efficiently and providing value to your customers.

Throughout this book, we'll be looking at both the startup and the ongoing operation of businesses. The strategy a business uses to make money will vary depending on whether the business is just starting or is operating in a mature, well-established industry.

Customer-Centric

New businesses and new products need a customer-centric focus. That is, the business should use strategies that focus on adding value for the customer. Customers purchase products because they receive a real or perceived value from them.

When a business is starting out, it should be in constant communication with its customers in an effort to determine how its products and services can be best tailored to meet the needs of its customers.

The business may excel at innovation and design. If so, the startup focus of the business should be directed toward identifying how its unique and innovative products can provide value to customers and identifying how to make money from the customer's purchases of these goods and services.

If the company excels at sales and marketing, the focus during startup should be on building brand recognition for the business's products and services and on identifying ways to get those products and services into the hands of customers so they can be purchased.

**A business that is able to CONTROL
its costs and PRODUCE more efficiently
than the competition will ACHIEVE
a COMPETITIVE advantage.**

If the business excels at customer service, the startup focus should be on building relationships with customers so they make initial as well as subsequent purchases, and recommend and refer the business to others.

The use of these strategies can create a competitive advantage for the business and allow it to price its products and services so it makes money.

When an operating business has existing customers, a customer-centric company will continue to focus on meeting the needs of its customers.

The business will continue to use its innovation and design, sales and marketing, or customer service strategies to offer products and services that provide value to its customers.

Many businesses that depend on trends, fashion, or technology must remain customer-centric, as the needs and desires of their customer are constantly changing as is the technology used in their products. The business must stay focused on the value to the customer and producing a positive customer experience.

Operational-Centric

In contrast to customer-centric businesses, operational-centric businesses make money by optimizing their operations and becoming low-cost producers. Operational-centric businesses sell the same products and services as the competition but are able to do so at a lower cost.

Operational-centric businesses are most often found in more mature, established industries. When a business introduces a new product or competes in a growing or changing industry, it is important to focus on the needs of the customer. The customer needs to be educated about the product, and the product needs to be sold to the customer.

As the demand for a product grows, the customer will no longer need to be educated about the product, and it will require less effort to sell it to the customer. New competitors will begin to enter the market, and the customer will begin to view the product as a commodity. The product's price will become a more important consideration than uniqueness, sales and marketing, and customer service.

At this point, a business selling this product will need to shift from customer-centric strategies to an operational-centric strategy. The business will make money by producing the product more efficiently than the competition.

A business that is able to control its costs and produce more efficiently than the competition will achieve a competitive advantage. An operational-centric business can use this competitive advantage to help the business make money.

Using Financial Statements

The financial operations of a business are reported in its financial statements. Financial statements tell a business's owners, investors and lenders whether or not the business is making money. They also tell the story of where and how a business is making money.

Financial statements can be analyzed to determine how effective the business has been in using its strategies to make money, and whether or not the business continues to have a competitive advantage.

To make money from a business over the long term, it's important that owners and managers understand the information contained in basic financial statements and how this information can be analyzed to help the business make money.

This book will teach you how to understand financial statements, and how to view and analyze the information to uncover the information that will help your business make money.

In other words, this book will teach you how to create and manage a profitable business.

CHAPTER TWO

Three Sample Companies

To understand the financial statements of a business and how it makes money, it is often helpful to visualize the information through the use of examples.

We've made this book as practical and useable as possible. Throughout the book, we will be presenting examples to help explain financial statement concepts and to help you understand how the knowledge of what these financial statements is telling you can help your business make money.

In this chapter, we'll present three sample companies that we'll be using as examples throughout the book. In general, businesses can be categorized either as manufacturing, retail or service. Using these categories, we've created a sample manufacturing company, a sample retail store, and a sample professional services business.

The differences and similarities between these different types of companies will be discussed in the chapters that follow. As you read this chapter and the ones that follow, we hope that you'll see your business in the examples and use the information to help your business make money.

Manufacturing Company: Boutique Handbags

Our sample manufacturing company presents an example of a simple manufacturing company, which we'll call Boutique Handbags. Most manufacturing companies face similar financial issues:

- Before a manufacturing business is able to make any products, it must create and equip a factory.
- The business must build its products before it can ship its products.
- The sales cycle for a manufacturing business might be six months between the manufacture of the product and the receipt of payment for the product.
- The business may have to pay its suppliers and workers before it receives payment from its customers.
- Cash will be needed to build the business and to sustain it between the manufacture of the products and receipt of payment for the products.

The Business

Boutique Handbags is a manufacturer of higher-end, designer women's handbags that are sold through women's specialty stores and select high-end department stores.

Boutique's handbags are made of bright, multicolored fabrics and come in a mix of colors and styles. Each of the fabric patterns is available for a limited time and a limited number of handbags with each pattern are produced. By restricting the production of any specific style and pattern, Boutique has an element of exclusivity for its products.

Boutique is a typical small manufacturer. The company founder, Ann Marie Williams, began sewing handbags by hand in her Vancouver home and selling them at arts and crafts festivals and trade shows. As the demand for her handbags grew, it became more difficult for Ann Marie to find the time or space in her home to manufacture the handbags, so Ann Marie has decided to move the company to an industrial park and purchase equipment and hire staff to assist in the production process.

With the move to the industrial park, the company will be able to focus on selling through retail outlets and stop attending arts and crafts festivals. Boutique can act as a manufacturer and distributor of the handbags to retail stores and stop direct sales to the public.

In addition to getting the business out of her house, formalizing the business structure will allow Ann Marie to spend time designing the upcoming season's handbags, and in a marketing role, meet with buyers and attend fashion and trade shows.

Ann Marie realized that to make sure she makes money from the new manufacturing facility, she would first have to develop financial projections for the business.

Product Sales

Ann Marie first looked at the revenue and production costs of the business. From her discussion with retail store buyers, she believes the handbags can be sold for an average retail price of $100 each and that the demand for the handbags will be 1,000 units per month.

From her study of the retail industry, Ann Marie knows that specialty department stores like to have a gross margin of approximately 60 percent on the items they sell. Based on this, Ann Marie estimates that if the retail price is $100 per unit, the retailers will be willing to pay Boutique $40 per handbag and still attain their required gross margin. Ann Marie decides on a per unit price to the retailers of $40 per handbag.

Ann Marie also estimates the costs of handbag production in the new manufacturing facility. Using the new cutting and sewing equipment in the facility, Ann Marie estimates that the labor costs to produce each handbag will be $12. Ann Marie also estimates that the materials for each handbag will cost $8. Each handbag will therefore cost Boutique $20 to produce.

If production costs $20 per handbag, and Boutique receives $40 from the sale of each handbag, Boutique will achieve a gross margin of 50 percent. Ann Marie knows from her research that a manufacturer's gross margin of 50 percent is typical for specialty manufacturers.

Operating Expenses

Ann Marie next looked at the business's operating expenses in the new facility. The first operating expense is rent. Boutique will be leasing manufacturing space in the industrial park for $2,000 per month. This space is sufficient not only for the handbag manufacturing process but also has room for a design studio and several small offices for Ann Marie and a bookkeeper/office manager.

Boutique will be responsible for paying the utility costs in its new facility. After discussions with the cutting and sewing equipment manufacturer and the local utility, Ann Marie estimates utilities will cost $1,500 per month.

To assist with the administration of the business, Ann Marie believes it will be necessary to hire office staff. After conversations with a local staffing agency, Ann Marie has estimated it will cost Boutique $2,500 per month to hire an individual to fill the role of bookkeeper and office manager. Additionally, Ann Marie will be receiving a salary of $4,000 per month for her role in running the company.

Ann Marie estimates that travel and marketing costs will be $1,500 per month for travel to and from trade shows and meetings with retail customers, and estimates a cost of $500 per month for outside accounting, payroll and legal services.

Startup Expenses

The last area Ann Marie looked at was startup expenses for the business. To meet the demand from the retailers and manufacture 1,000 handbags per month, Boutique must invest in two advanced cutting and sewing machines. These machines can be purchased at a cost of $10,000 each.

Additionally, Ann Marie feels it will be necessary to invest in systems and software to assist in inventory tracking and accounting. She estimates a purchase cost of $6,000. She also believes it will cost $4,000 to equip and set up the office and design area in the new facility.

Business Cash Flow

The final consideration for Boutique Handbags is the amount of cash the business will need to pay its bills as it starts up operations. From her past experience, Ann Marie knows that the timing of revenue and expense cash flows is an important consideration in developing forecasts for a business.

It typically takes retailers 60 days to pay Boutique for the handbags. Boutique is obligated to pay its suppliers for the materials used in the manufacture of the handbags in 30 days, so Ann Marie immediately realizes she has a mismatch in the timing of Boutique's receivables and payables.

Additionally, the labor costs of manufacturing the handbags are due to the employees in the month in which the bags are made, so Ann Marie recognizes there's also a cash flow timing issue here. She also realizes that the operating expenses of the business must be paid each month regardless of when the retailers pay Boutique for the handbags, and that it might take a month or more to move the equipment in and set up the new facility before any manufacturing can take place.

Finally, Ann Marie realizes that before the products can be shipped to the retailers, they must first be manufactured and temporarily stored in inventory.

After reviewing this information, Ann Marie realizes that it might be four months from the time a handbag begins the manufacturing process until cash is received from the retailer.

Issues Unique to Manufacturers

In this book, we'll use Boutique Handbags as an example of a typical small manufacturer. We'll discuss some of the issues that Boutique faced when they moved from a homebased business to a manufacturing facility. Typical of many manufacturers, Boutique has had to invest in machinery for use in the production process, and hire and train staff to manufacture the handbags. Boutique also must incur costs to manufacture its products many months in advance of receiving payments for these products. It must also keep a significant amount of cash in the business to pay for things like rent and employee wages while its products are in inventory or awaiting sale at a retailer.

Professional Service Firm: Uptown Chiropractic

Our sample professional service example is Uptown Chiropractic. Uptown Chiropractic will focus on the financial issues affecting many professional service businesses, including:

- The business has no inventory.
- The business provides services rather than sells products.
- Revenue may be received months after the services are provided.
- Employee costs are a significant part of the business's expenses.
- The business has a choice of using the cash or accrual method of accounting.

The Business

Uptown Chiropractic is a small chiropractic office located in a medical office building in Alexandria, Virginia. The office furnishes a full range of chiropractic services, including treatment for back and neck stiffness, leg and arm pain, slipped disks, headaches, whiplash, and sports injuries.

Uptown Chiropractic is owned by Dr. Eric Press. Dr. Press is an experienced chiropractor who recently left a multidoctor chiropractic office to open his own practice. Dr. Press is the primary treating chiropractor in the office. The office is open six days a week, from 10 am to 5 pm Monday through Friday and 9 am to noon on Saturdays.

The chief costs are the WAGES and SALARIES paid to the staff who provides services to the customers.

Uptown Chiropractic's office includes three treatment rooms, an exam room, a waiting room, and a small office for Dr. Press. The exam room includes a full array of diagnostic equipment, and each treatment room is equipped with muscle stimulation equipment, hot packs and ultrasound equipment.

In a medical practice, as in many service businesses, the chief costs are the wages and salaries paid to the staff who provides services to the customers. These costs are typically reflected on the income statement as cost of services provided, or COS.

In developing his business plan for Uptown Chiropractic, Dr. Press analyzed the services to be provided and concluded that the office would need a chiropractic doctor and two assistants to provide services to the patients as well as part-time staff to handle bookkeeping and billing activities.

The specialized annual accounting functions and weekly payroll could be obtained from outside services very cost-effectively, so this expertise wouldn't be needed in the office.

Services

Dr. Press will fill the role of primary treating chiropractor in the office. He estimates he'll be able to spend 50 percent of his time treating patients, 30 percent of his time on insurance company-related paperwork, and 20 percent of his time marketing and administering the business. Dr. Press believes he should be able to treat 400 patients per month. Based on a typical salary for a chiropractor, Dr. Press estimates his pay at $60,000 per year ($5,000 per month).

The two full-time chiropractic assistants will perform a variety of duties in the office associated with patient care and record-keeping. These duties will range from answering the phone and scheduling appointments, to taking patient health histories and preparing insurance forms, to assisting with patient treatment. Dr. Press has identified two excellent chiropractic assistants willing to join his staff. One has more than 10 years of experience and is willing to work for a salary of $30,000 per year ($2,500 per month). The other only has six months of experience and will work for a salary of $24,000 per year ($2,000 per month).

In addition to the salaries, a chiropractic office incurs some small costs for medical supplies associated with patient treatments. Dr. Press has estimated these at $2,000 per month and is treating these expenses as a cost of services.

Operations

The part-time bookkeeper will assist in the business's record-keeping. The billing specialist will help prepare documents for submission to the insurance companies and track the status of bills submitted for reimbursement. These services are expected to cost $1,500 per month.

Dr. Press plans to include both the cost of his salary as well as that of the chiropractic assistants under cost of services on the profit and loss statement since these costs are directly related to patient care. He plans to include the bookkeeper and billing specialist costs as operating expenses since these are not related to patient care.

The other costs incurred by Uptown Chiropractic are office operating expenses. In addition to the aforementioned $1,500 per month for the bookkeeper and billing specialist, other costs include $2,000 for monthly office rent, $1,000 for utilities, $500 per month budgeted for ongoing training to maintain professional certification, and $500 per month budgeted for accounting, payroll and legal services.

Finally, to reduce the upfront costs associated with opening a medical office, Dr. Press has chosen to lease the medical equipment for the treatment and exam rooms. He has been able to lease the necessary equipment from a medical supply company at a cost of $4,500 per month. After consulting with his accountant, Dr. Press has decided it would be best to treat the lease cost as an operating expense since it must be paid regardless of patient volume.

Startup Expenses

The only out-of-pocket expenses required to start the business are $5,000 for computers and software, and $5,000 to purchase furniture for his office, the reception desk and the waiting area.

Business Cash Flow

Like most medical practices, Uptown Chiropractic treats a significant number of clients whose medical bills are paid by their insurance companies. The insurance companies tend to reimburse at rates that are lower than those paid by cash customers.

Uptown Chiropractic receives an average payment of $55 per treatment from the insurance companies vs. an average payment of $75 per treatment from its cash customers. Dr. Press estimates that 25 percent of his business will be cash, while 75 percent will be dependent on insurance company reimbursement.

Additionally, while the cash customers pay at the time of treatment, insurance company reimbursement is received in an average of 120 days.

The business must pay the operating expenses and salaries of Dr. Press and the chiropractic assistants each month, even if they haven't received payment from the insurance companies.

Issues Unique to Professional Services

A medical practice, such as Uptown Chiropractic, is similar in many ways to many other professional service firms, such as law practices, accounting firms, and consultancies. The company is essentially selling the owners' and the associates' time. The company doesn't manufacture products or carry inventory, and the business's primary operating costs are staffing related. The other operating expenses are small relative to staffing costs. The key to profitability for this type of business is generating an adequate volume of customers so that sufficient revenue can be generated to cover salary costs and operating expenses.

Retail Store: Bonnie's Beachwear

Our sample retail store is Bonnie's Beachwear. This company will be used to discuss the financial issues affecting retail businesses. These issues can include:

- The need to purchase inventory to stock the store before any sales can be made
- The need to sell inventory to generate revenue to pay suppliers, salaries and operating expenses
- Timing differences between when revenue is received and when expenses must be paid
- The effects of spoilage, changing trends and price discounting on profitability

The Business

Bonnie's Beachwear is a women's retail store located in a busy shopping district across the street from the beach in Miami's trendy South Beach neighborhood.

Bonnie's shop specializes in the sale of women's bathing suits, coverups and casual beachwear. Bonnie's customers include wealthier residents from the Miami area as well as a significant number of tourists staying at nearby hotels. Bonnie's typical customer is a fashion-conscious woman with a desire to wear the latest designs while at the beach.

The business must GENERATE sufficient SALES revenue to cover its monthly expenses.

The owner of Bonnie's Beachwear, Bonnie Bradley, began the business several years ago after working for many years as a women's apparel manager for a major retail chain. Bonnie began the business after receiving an early retirement package from her employer. After extensive research into several retail opportunities, Bonnie decided to open a beachwear shop specializing in mid- and higher-priced women's beachwear because she had experience with this market from her corporate life and because of the potential profits an efficiently run store offers the owner.

In looking for a location for the business, she first determined that beachwear sales tended to be higher in resort locations that are warm year-round and where there are many tourists who are potential customers for beachwear. Because of the emphasis on tourists, she also determined that she should locate the shop in an area where the tourists were likely to be, such as near the beach or in the hotel district.

After investigating several locations, she settled on the South Beach neighborhood of Miami, a year-round tourist destination, with a famous beach, many hotels and an existing shopping district. After visiting the area and observing the shoppers and flow of foot traffic, Bonnie identified a vacant retail unit on the main drag across the street from the beach, on a block bounded by two art-deco hotels. Bonnie felt it was the perfect location for her business and leased the space for $3,000 per month.

Overall, Bonnie felt that being located in Miami would be an advantage for the business. The year-round warm weather and continual flow of tourists creates a constant demand for beachwear. This creates a much more consistent revenue stream for the business, which allows Bonnie to pay a high rent and keep the staff busy year-round.

Product Sales

As is the case for many clothing retailers, it's important that Bonnie's Beachwear stock the latest beachwear fashions so customers can purchase current designs and have reason to visit the store more frequently to see what's new.

Beachwear that has gone out of style is often difficult to sell, and retailers often must discount older inventory heavily. To avoid such problems, it's important for retailers such as Bonnie's Beachwear to stay abreast of current fashion trends and stock the latest inventory.

Designers introduce the new season's beachwear styles at their annual fall fashion shows. By introducing the styles in the fall, the designers are able to accept orders and manufacture the beachwear for the busy summer beach season. Bonnie typically attends several of these fashion shows and prepares her inventory orders following these shows to include the styles she believes will be most likely to sell.

The emphasis on fashion will allow Bonnie to sell the beachwear at a premium price, from $25 to $100. Based on her past retail experience, Bonnie expected to sell more of the lower priced items and fewer of the higher priced items. She estimated the average sale at $50. From her discussions with beachwear distributors and fashion designers, she determined the business could expect to purchase beachwear items for the store at an average wholesale price of $18 per item.

At these price points, Bonnie's Beachwear would earn a gross margin of 64 percent. A gross margin of this size is typical of higher-end and specialty retailers, such as Bonnie's Beachwear.

Startup Expenses

By opening an upscale store in a prime location, Bonnie realized her operating expenses would be more than if the store were located in a nonprime location. In addition to rent, she knew she would have to spend money to outfit the shop for a wealthier customer by including upscale fitting rooms, higher-end merchandise displays, and carpeting and wood furniture throughout. Bonnie estimated it would cost $40,000 to outfit the store.

She also budgeted an additional $10,000 startup expense for the purchase of computerized cash registers, and an office computer and inventory management software.

Operations

Additionally, Bonnie knew she could not spend all her time in the store waiting on customers. She would need to divide her time between managing the store, meeting with vendors, and marketing the business. Fashion trends in beachwear are continually changing so Bonnie will also need to devote some of her time to attending beachwear fashion shows to keep on top of the latest beachwear styles.

In order to accomplish this, Bonnie planned to hire sales staff to wait on customers and handle the cash registers. Because of the focus on a higher-end customer, Bonnie knew she couldn't just hire inexperienced, minimum-wage workers. She would need experienced salespeople and would have to pay higher wages to attract this staff. She estimated an hourly wage of $12 to

$15 per hour. Assuming she always had two salespeople in the store, she estimated a sales staff expense of $10,000 per month.

In addition to rental and staff expenses, Bonnie estimated her utility costs at $1,500. She also planned to spend $2,000 per month to advertise the business and budgeted $1,000 for outside services to help with accounting and payroll.

Finally, she budgeted $4,500 per month as her salary. Overall, Bonnie estimated monthly operating expenses of $22,000 for the business and $50,000 in startup costs.

Business Cash Flow

Bonnie recalled her experiences with starting new retail stores for her former employer. She realized there could be a several-month lag between the time the store was leased and renovated for her business, and the time her first customers made their purchases. During this time, the space would have to be renovated and the merchandise display racks purchased and installed. Additionally, she would have to order inventory to fill the store prior to its grand opening, and she might have to pay for some or all of this inventory before the store opened. Although she was projecting robust sales for the store, Bonnie realized that sales volume during the first few months might be low, as it would take time for word of the shop to build.

Issues Unique to Retail Stores

In this book, we'll use Bonnie's Beachwear as an example of a typical small retailer. The issues Bonnie's faces are similar to those that any small retailer or restaurant might face in beginning operations. The business has to find and rent a location for the business, invest in renovating the space, outfit the store to display its merchandise, and purchase inventory—all before it can open its doors to the public. As is the case with most retail and food-service businesses, Bonnie's makes a small amount of profit on each sale, yet incurs significant fixed operating expenses each month. The business must generate sufficient sales revenue to cover its monthly expenses.

Throughout this book, we'll use the business activities of these three companies as examples as we build financial statements, analyze financial operations, and evaluate strategies and competitive advantage.

Part Two

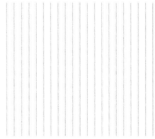

Financial Statements

The financial results of a business are expressed through financial statements. In order to gain an understanding of finance and obtain the knowledge essential to the use of finance as a tool for your business, it's necessary to acquire a basic understanding of financial terminology and financial statements.

In this part of the book, we explain the structure and content of three key financial statements—the cash flow statement, the profit and loss statement and the balance sheet—and demonstrate how different business activities are reflected on financial statements using the operations of our sample companies as examples.

Part 2 provides the basic information necessary to understand the cash flow, profits, and assets and liabilities of your business.

CHAPTER THREE

Cash Flow Statement: The Basics

The cash flow statement is one of three primary types of financial statements. The other two are the profit and loss statement and the balance sheet.

We'll discuss the cash flow statement first because in many ways the cash flow statement is the simplest and most understandable of the three financial statements.

It is also one of the most important financial statements. A business pays its bills with cash, and the cash flow statement tells a business where cash is coming from and where it is being spent. If a business is consistently spending more cash than it takes in, it will eventually go broke. Therefore, it's critical for a business to understand the cash that it is taking in and the cash that it is spending.

What Is Cash?

Let's start with the definition of cash: Cash is the amount of paper currency and coins, checks to be deposited, and bank balances the business owns.

In the ancient world, business transactions were conducted using currency. Buyers and sellers physically carried around bags of coins and used these coins to complete their transactions. Of course, bags of coins aren't the easiest things to carry around, and there's always the risk of loss or theft.

With the advent of a stable banking system in the mid-20th century, checks replaced coins and paper currency as the norm for many transactions. Consumers had the option of paying for their purchases with paper currency or with a check. Merchants could take their checks to the bank and redeem them for cash, or more likely deposit them into their checking accounts so they had cash available to pay their suppliers for the merchandise they just sold.

If a business is consistently SPENDING MORE cash than it TAKES IN, it will eventually GO BROKE.

Checks offered a way to transact business without the need for carrying bags of currency (and all of the associated risks), and to allow transactions to be completed via the mail. No need to physically visit the landlord to pay the rent, just put a check in the mail.

The key drawback to the use of checks was the time it took a check to "clear the bank." That is, the time it took the seller's bank to collect the money from the buyer's bank and deposit it into the seller's account. This "float" period could take a week or more during which time neither the buyer nor seller had access to the money. Additionally, there was always the risk of a "bad check," where the buyer wrote a check for more money than he had in the bank.

During the later part of the 20th century, the use of electronic funds began to replace checks as the primary means of conducting business. Electronic funds are becoming a very important way to conduct business in today's world.

One example would be when a customer uses a debit card to pay for a product or service. The funds to pay for the product or service are transferred from the customer's bank or credit union account to the business's bank or credit union account within a few days.

Similarly, when a customer uses a credit card to make a purchase, the credit card processing company (MasterCard, Visa, American Express, Discover, etc.) deposits the funds into the seller's bank account within a few days.

This all takes place electronically. The merchant doesn't have to take checks to the bank or wait for checks to clear the bank, and there's no risk of taking a bad check. Of course the financial institutions—banks, credit unions, and credit card companies (and even PayPal)—generally charge a fee for this service.

Many businesses have progressed to the point where they do not even accept currency any more. Many internet purchases are transacted solely using electronic funds, requiring the buyer to use a credit or debit card for payment. And if you've flown on an airplane recently, you may have heard the announcement that they're now only able to accept credit and debit cards for in-flight services, such as drinks, meals or headsets.

Many smaller businesses use PayPal as a means of payment for their goods and services. PayPal is an electronic payment service geared for small businesses that deducts the money directly from the buyer's bank account and moves it to the seller's bank account.

Even the government has gotten into the act. It is now possible for your individual tax refund to be deposited directly into your bank account. No more waiting for your refund check to arrive or worrying that it has been lost in the mail.

It's also possible for a business to make its payroll and income tax payments to the IRS and to its state tax department electronically, using nothing more than a bank account, computer and internet connection. The business logs onto the IRS or state tax department website and initiates an electronic transfer from the business bank account directly to the federal and state coffers. The IRS doesn't want to wait for you to write a check or to mail it, either. In fact, for businesses in which annual payroll or income tax payments exceed a threshold, the IRS requires that the payments be made electronically.

Let's go back to the definition of cash: Cash is the amount of paper currency and coins, checks to be deposited, and bank balances that the business owns.

This definition includes the three types of cash discussed above: The actual currency—the dollar bills and coins—in the cash drawer, in the bank bag ready for deposit to the bank, or in the safe in the back room; the checks the business has received but has not yet deposited in the bank or that have not yet cleared the bank; and the balances on deposit with the bank, credit union, or other financial institution that can be readily withdrawn. This is the cash a business has available to pay its bills and its owners.

When STARTING OUT, most businesses use MORE CASH than they take in.

Of course, not all businesses deal in all three types of cash. Typically, only retail businesses deal with currency. Many retail customers continue to use currency to pay for products and services offered by retail businesses. Retail businesses, in turn, need to keep some currency on hand to make change, or because the currency hasn't yet been deposited in the bank.

Larger businesses, and retail establishments that accept credit and debit cards for transactions, are the prime users of electronic fund payments, where the cash is moved to and from their bank accounts without ever having been in currency or check form.

Many other small and medium-size businesses, particularly nonretail businesses, continue to use checks as a means of paying for goods and services purchased, and to receive checks as payment for goods and services sold. However, in the internet world, even small businesses use electronic payment systems.

When you add all these up, this is the "cash" the business has for its operations.

Understanding the Cash Flow Statement

During any month, a business will have inflows and outflows of cash. The purpose of the cash flow statement is to show how much cash a business starts with at the beginning of the month, how much cash the business takes in and how much it pays out, and the cash left over at the end of the month. Typically, cash flow statements are done monthly, although a cash flow statement can be done for a whole year or even daily.

Most businesses begin with at least some cash. This cash may be kept as a reserve, to buy inventory, or to pay expenses during the month. When starting out, most businesses use more cash than they take in.

Let's look at the "Simple Cash Flow Statement" below.

Simple Cash Flow Statement	
Cash at Beginning of Month	**$500**
Cash Received During Month	$5,000
Cash Paid During Month	$4,000
Cash at End of Month	**$1,500**

Our business starts the month with $500 in cash. During the month it takes in $5,000 in cash and pays out $4,000 in cash, so it ends the month with $1,500 in cash ($500 + $5,000 - $4,000 = $1,500).

This is the concept of a cash flow statement. How much cash did the business start with, how much did it take in, how much did it spend, and how much does it have at the end of the period.

In our simple example, the business appears to be doing well. It started the month with $500, took in more cash than it spent, and ended the month with $1,500.

This simple cash flow statement presents the concept of a cash flow statement, but it doesn't tell us what's behind the numbers. Why did the business take in $5,000 in cash? What were the sources of the cash? Was it all sales, or did the owner invest additional money in the business? Were the sales all from this period, or does the cash flow include collections from prior periods?

What is behind the $4,000 in cash paid out? Did the cash payments include all the current period expenses, or did the business defer paying some bills, or pay some bills from a prior period?

For the answers to these questions, we'll need a more detailed cash flow statement.

Cash Flow at Bonnie's Beachwear

Let's take a look at the monthly cash flow for one of our sample companies, Bonnie's Beachwear. We'll use Bonnie's business to build a more detailed cash flow statement that shows us what's behind the numbers.

Recall from Chapter 2, where we introduced our sample companies, that Bonnie's Beachwear is a women's specialty retailer selling beachwear from a shop in a busy shopping district across from Miami's South Beach. The business generates revenue by selling bathing suits, coverups, and casual beachwear to a customer base that includes tourists and area residents.

Bonnie's Beachwear makes money by purchasing its product at an average wholesale cost of $18, then selling it at an average retail price of $50. Her store sells enough beachwear each month so that the business is able to pay the business's monthly operating expenses.

Bonnie's Beachwear receives cash during the month in several ways. First, customers make purchases in the store using cash (currency and coins). At the end of each day, the business deposits the cash from these purchases in the bank.

Second, Bonnie's Beachwear allows customers to write checks for their purchases. At the end of each day, the business also deposits these checks in the bank. It typically takes Bonnie's bank from three days to a week to clear the checks from the customers' banks and make the cash available in Bonnie's accounts.

Finally, Bonnie's Beachwear allows customers to pay with credit and debit cards. As each transaction is processed at the cash register, a request is generated within the MasterCard or Visa processing system to charge the customer for the transaction and to deposit the cash into Bonnie's Beachwear's bank account. Within a few days, the funds are electronically transferred and the cash is available to the business.

Examining the Cash Flow Statement

During the month, Bonnie's Beachwear has two types of cash activities: It receives cash in payment for the merchandise it sold, and it spends cash to pay suppliers for this merchandise and to pay operating expenses. Let's start by looking at the cash it receives.

Cash Received

Assuming Bonnie's Beachwear sold $50,000 worth of merchandise in a month, the cash received section of the cash flow statement could be as follows:

Bonnie's Beachwear Monthly Cash Receipts

Cash Received During Month

Cash Sales	$5,000
Collections from Check Sales	$5,000
Collections from Credit and Debit Sales	$40,000
Total Cash Received During Month	**$50,000**

The business received $5,000 in cash from cash sales, received an additional $5,000 in cash from sales to customers who wrote checks, and received $40,000 in cash from electronic funds transfers from customers who paid with credit or debit cards.

Cash Paid

Retail businesses, such as Bonnie's Beachwear, use cash to pay bills associated with two major categories each month: the costs of purchasing the merchandise that is sold to the customers, and the costs of operating the store. The operating expenses of the store include paying employees, rent, utilities, and advertising and administrative expenses.

In the case of Bonnie's Beachwear, if $50,000 worth of merchandise were sold during the month, the purchase of the merchandise would have cost the business $18,000. If the operating expenses for the month were $22,000, the cash paid section of the cash flow statement would look as follows:

Bonnie's Beachwear Monthly Cash Payments

Cash Paid During Month	
Merchandise Purchased for Resale	$18,000
Operating Expenses	
Rent	$3,000
Utilities	$1,500
Sales Staff Salaries	$10,000
Owners' Salary	$4,500
Advertising	$2,000
Accounting, Payroll and Legal	$1,000
Total Operating Expenses	$22,000
Total Cash Paid During Month	**$40,000**

As you can see, during the month, Bonnie's Beachwear made a total of $40,000 in cash payments.

Putting It Together

The monthly cash flow statement combines the cash the business had on hand at the beginning of the month with the cash received and cash paid sections, and shows the monthly cash flow and cash position at the end of the month.

Bonnie's Beachwear Monthly Cash Flow Statement

Cash at Beginning of Month	**$5,000**
Cash Received During Month	
Cash Sales	$5,000
Collections from Check Sales	$5,000
Collections from Credit and Debit Sales	$40,000
Total Cash Received During Month	**$50,000**
Cash Paid During Month	
Merchandise Purchased for Resale	$18,000
Operating Expenses	
Rent	$3,000
Utilities	$1,500
Sales Staff Salaries	$10,000
Owners' Salary	$4,500
Advertising	$2,000
Accounting, Payroll and Legal	$1,000
Total Operating Expenses	$22,000
Total Cash Paid During Month	**$40,000**
Cash at End of Month	**$15,000**

In our example (see page 39), we see that Bonnie's Beachwear began the month with $5,000 in cash, got paid by its customers, paid its bills, and ended the month with $15,000 in cash, a gain $10,000.

In looking at the cash flow statement, we're also able to see that the gain in cash came from the operation of the business. The owner didn't put any of her own funds into the business during the month nor did the business borrow any money during the month. These would each be reflected as cash received on the cash flow statement had they occurred.

During the month, the business generated cash from its operations. Not all businesses, particularly startup ventures, are able to do this consistently. Additionally, as businesses expand, they have a tendency to use more cash. That's why understanding the cash flow of the business is critical to making money.

CHAPTER FOUR

Organize Your Cash Flow by Activity

 One of the keys to understanding a business's cash flow is to understand why the cash was received and why it was paid.

Cash flow activity can be divided into three categories: operating cash flow, asset activity cash flow, and financing activity cash flow. Each of these categories represents a different type of activity that generates cash for the business and uses cash.

In this chapter, we'll look at each of these categories individually and what they represent in a cash flow statement. (See page 42 for an example of a cash flow statement for Bonnie's Beachwear, where the various cash flows have been organized by category and activity.)

Bonnie's Beachwear Monthly Cash Flow Statement Organized by Type of Cash Flow

Cash at Beginning of Month	**$5,000**
Cash Received	
Cash Received from Operating Activities	
Cash Sales	$5,000
Credit/Debit Card Sales	$5,000
Collections of Accounts Receivable	$40,000
Total Cash Received from Operating Activities	**$50,000**
Cash Received from Asset Activities	
Cash Received from Asset Sales	$0
Total Cash Received from Asset Activities	**$0**
Cash Received from Financing Activities	
Owners' Investment	$20,000
Equity Investors	$0
Loans and Other Borrowings	$25,000
Total Cash Received from Financing Activities	**$45,000**
Total Cash Received	**$95,000**
Cash Paid	
Cash Used in Operating Activities	
Inventory Purchases	$18,000
Raw Material Purchases	$0
Payment of Accounts Payable	$0
Selling Expenses	$11,000
General and Administrative Expenses	$11,000
Research and Development	$0
Total Cash Used in Operating Activities	**$40,000**
Cash Used for Asset Activities	
Equipment Purchases	$10,000
Other Asset Purchases	$40,000
Total Cash Used for Asset Activities	**$50,000**
Cash Used in Financing Activities	
Interest Payments on Loans	$500
Principal Payments on Loans	$0
Payments to Owners	$0
Total Cash Used in Financing Activities	**$500**
Total Cash Paid	**$90,500**
Cash at End of Month	**$9,500**

Operating Cash Flow

A profitable business generates cash from its operations. That is, from selling products and services to the public or to other businesses. To generate a profit, the business must be able to pay its operating expenses as well as pay the suppliers and workers who produce the products and supply the services.

The cash generated from the sale of products and services is known as cash received from operating activities. Cash that's used to pay for the products and services sold and to pay for the ongoing operations of the business is known as cash used in operating activities. Operating cash flow includes all the cash in and out of the business related to the actual operations of the business.

A PROFITABLE business generates cash from its operations.

In the case of Bonnie's Beachwear, the business sold a variety of bathing suits and beachwear products to the public from a retail store. The purchase of these items by Bonnie's customers generate cash for the business. In our sample cash flow statement (on page 42), Bonnie's received $50,000 in cash from these operating activities.

But Bonnie's Beachwear also has expenses. The bathing suits and other beachwear products must be purchased from manufacturers. Additionally, the business incurs a monthly cost to operate the retail store, including paying rent and staff salaries. Paying for these items is a use of the business's cash. In our example, Bonnie's used $40,000 of cash in its operating activities.

In order for a business to generate operating cash flow, it will almost always have spent some money to purchase assets that are used in operations. Asset purchases are captured in the asset activity section of the cash flow statement.

Asset Activity Cash Flow

Asset activity refers to the purchase and sale of assets by the business. Asset activity cash flow includes any new assets purchased by the business that are used in its production processes as well as the sale of old assets the business no longer needs.

Most businesses use some type of assets in their operations. For instance, retail stores such as Bonnie's Beachwear typically would need to purchase the furniture used in the store as well as the racks and shelving used to display the merchandise for sale to customers. They might also have purchased cash registers, computers, and software that allow them to track inventory and manage the business's books.

> **Even SIMPLE BUSINESSES such as home repair contractors need to PURCHASE ASSETS to be used in the business.**

As we discussed in Chapter 2, Bonnie's Beachwear spent $40,000 to renovate and outfit the store and another $10,000 to purchase cash registers, computers and software. These purchases are shown as cash used for asset activities on the cash flow statement.

But it's not only retailers that need to purchase assets to be used in operations. Manufacturing firms need to purchase the equipment and machinery that allows them to produce their products. In the example of our manufacturing business, Boutique Handbags purchased cutting and sewing machinery to be used in the production of the handbags. Asset purchases by manufacturing companies can include everything from simple machinery to fully equipped factories.

Even simple businesses such as home repair contractors need to purchase assets to be used in the business. A good example is the truck used by a construction contractor, as well as the hammers, saws and other tools the contractor might use in performing his work.

Cash used to purchase these assets is referred to as cash used for asset activities. Cash received from the sale of any of these assets is referred to as cash from asset activities.

Most businesses at one time or another need to purchase assets to be used in production processes. This often occurs at business startup and at select times during the life of the business. Obtaining the cash to purchase the assets is often the result of financing activity.

Financing Activity Cash Flow

Financing activity cash flow includes cash that comes to the business as a result of financing or investment activities or that is used by the business to pay lenders or investors.

Financing activity cash flow includes:

- Investments made in the business by owners and equity investors

- The proceeds from loans and other financing received by the business

- Dividends and other payments made to investors

- The repayment of loans and other financing

In our Bonnie's Beachwear example, let's assume that Bonnie invested $20,000 of her own money to help start the business and obtained a bank loan for $25,000. These are shown as cash received from financing activities on the cash flow statement.

Additionally, since Bonnie's borrowed money from the bank, the business will have to pay interest on this money. The interest payments to the bank ($500 in this example) appear as cash used for financing activities on the cash flow statement.

Financing activity cash flow is critically important for a business. Financing activities are typically a major source of cash for a business, particularly for asset purchases and startup funds. At times, financing activity cash flow can exceed the cash flow from operations.

It's important to note that a business doesn't make money from financing activities. However, excessive financing activities can make a business that's not profitable appear to have sufficient cash flow. For that reason, it's critical that the operating cash flows and financing activity cash flows be listed separately and reviewed separately on a cash flow statement. A business that's not profitable from operations can still have a positive cash flow if the owners continue to invest in the business or if the business is borrowing heavily.

The key to creating a PROFITABLE BUSINESS involves generating cash from operating activities.

Over the long-term, a business that must rely on loans and additional investment by the owners, but that's not profitable from operations, is not a sustainable business. At some point, the owners' willingness to invest or the banks willingness to loan will cease and the business will be left short of cash.

Financing activity is best used by businesses for specific purposes such as the payment of startup expenses, the purchase of assets for the production process, or as a source of working capital. (Working capital will be discussed further in Chapter 11.)

As you can see, a business can receive cash from several different types of activities and spend cash on several different types of activities. Distinguishing the source of your cash is important, since the key to creating a profitable business involves generating cash from operating activities—that is, receiving payments from customers and not from loans or the sale of assets.

CHAPTER FIVE

Profit and Loss Statement Basics

Now that you understand the role of the cash flow statement, let's take a look at another primary financial statement—the profit and loss statement. The profit and loss statement plays a very important role: It tells you and your investors whether or not your business is making money.

Profit Is an Estimate

Before we explore how to create and use the profit and loss statement, a bit of background on its origin and terminology is in order.

A profit and loss statement is an accounting statement. It's typically developed by accountants (or by your accounting software), using the rules of accounting.

Whereas the cash flow statement measures the actual flow of cash to and from the business, a profit and loss statement estimates a business's profits (or income) based on the rules of accounting. Although accounting is often presented as an exact science, accounting numbers are often estimates, based on the business owners' and accountants' best guess as to how and when financial events occurred. For example, consider our manufacturing company, Boutique Handbags, which manufactures handbags and sells them to retail stores. In the normal course of business, the process of selling these handbags might go something like this:

- On March 15, a retail store calls Boutique Handbags and places an order for several cases of handbags.

- Boutique Handbags manufactures the handbags, packages them, and ships them to the retail store on April 5.

- Once the retail store receives the handbags, it's generally allowed some time before it has to pay Boutique Handbags for the product. This could be 30 or 60 days, so Boutique Handbags might not receive payment until June 5.

The accountant preparing Boutique Handbags' profit and loss statement must make a determination as to when the "sale" occurred. Did the sale occur when the retail store placed the order, when the products were shipped, or when payment was received?

Under the rules of accounting, the accountant would generally say the sale occurred when the retail store placed the order, so when the profit and loss statement is prepared for March 31, the accountant would include the revenue from the sale even though the company hadn't yet received the cash.

This is just one example of how accounting rules can affect a company's profit and loss statement. Throughout this chapter, we'll point out how these rules affect the elements of the profit and loss statement.

From our handbag example, you can see that a key element in a profit and loss statement is recognizing when revenue and expense events occur. Keep this in mind as you read our discussion of the profit and loss statement.

Chapter 6 includes a full discussion of how the income of a business differs from the cash flows of a business. Chapter 20 discusses some of the different accounting rules and how these can affect a business.

BY ANY OTHER NAME

The profit and loss statement is known by several names. In addition to the profit and loss statement, it's also commonly referred to as a *P&L statement*. Other times, it's known by names such as an *income statement, statement of earnings, statement of operations, operating statement*, or *revenue and expense statement*.

The use of multiple terms to describe the same thing is one of the most common problems people have in understanding financial statements. At times, it seems like accountants invent fancy terms to describe the same information in an effort to add mystique to their profession. The reality is more complicated as the varying terminology has developed over time from usage in different countries, regions and companies.

Throughout this book, we'll be consistent in our use of terms. For instance, the profit and loss statement will always be referred to as the profit and loss statement; we won't confuse the issue by using any of the other names. In these "By Any Other Name" boxes, we'll provide an explanation when multiple terms can be used for the same thing.

The use of multiple terms doesn't stop with the name of the statement itself. Many of the line items on a profit and loss statement go by multiple names as well. These will be explained as the terms are encountered.

Understanding the Profit and Loss Statement

The concept of a profit and loss statement is very simple. A profit and loss statement compares a business's revenue and expenses. If revenue exceeds expenses, the business is making money. If expenses exceed revenue, the business isn't making money.

In the terminology of the profit and loss statement, if revenue exceeds expenses, the business has a positive net profit, and if expenses exceed revenue, the business has a negative net profit, or a net loss. Here is an example of a simple profit and loss statement:

Profit and Loss Statement Summary

Revenue	$100,000
Less Expenses	$89,600
Net Profit	**$10,400**

In practice, of course, the profit and loss statement is a bit more complicated. Fortunately, much like the cash flow statement, the profit and loss statement can be divided into sections based on activities.

There are three primary categories of revenue and expenses:

1. The revenue and expenses directly associated with sales activities (i.e., selling goods and services to customers).

2. The ongoing expenses of operating the business and repaying any loans.

3. Any one-time, nonoperating income and expenses.

In the remainder of this chapter, we'll discuss how a business's sales activities and operating activities are reflected on the profit and loss statement. One-time, nonoperating income and expense items are best left to a more advanced accounting book.

Examining the Profit and Loss Statement

Let's look at each of the key components of a profit and loss statement. We'll be building the profit and loss statement as we progress through the chapter.

Sales Activities

The sales activities section of the profit and loss statement includes all revenue a business generates from selling goods and services, as well as the expenses associated with selling those goods and services.

Revenue

A business earns revenue by selling goods or services to the public or to other businesses.

In the sample businesses presented in Chapter 2, Bonnie's Beachwear sells bathing suits and other beach apparel (goods) to the public through her retail store. Boutique Handbags manufactures handbags (goods) and sells them to stores that then sell them to the public.

In contrast, Uptown Chiropractic doesn't manufacture products or sell goods to the public. The business earns revenue by providing services to patients in the form of chiropractic treatments.

BY ANY OTHER NAME

On the profit and loss statement, revenue can also be called *sales*. When business owners talk about revenue or sales, they're talking about the same thing—the money the business generates from selling goods and services.

Throughout this book, we will use the term "revenue" to mean the money the business generates from selling goods and services, after accounting for any returns that may have taken place. As discussed in the "Profit Is an Estimate" section, accounting rules determine when a business recognizes revenue on its profit and loss statement. Under accounting rules, manufacturers and retail businesses typically recognize revenue when the sale is made, regardless of when they actually receive the cash.

However, service businesses have a choice as to when they recognize revenue. Some service businesses will recognize revenue when the contract is signed or the service is provided, while others may wait until the cash is received to recognize the revenue.

In accounting terms, a business that recognizes revenue when a sale is made uses what's known as accrual accounting while a business that recognizes revenue when the cash is received uses cash accounting. When a business recognizes its revenue has an impact on its profit and loss statement.

The concepts of cash and accrual accounting are discussed more fully in Chapter 20.

Cost of Goods Sold

As we stated earlier, there are two primary types of expenses businesses incur: those that are associated with purchasing or producing the goods and services that are sold to customers, and the ongoing expenses of operating the business (also referred to as operating expenses). Cost of goods sold is an example of the former type. We'll talk about operating expenses later on.

Retail and manufacturing businesses typically include an expense line for cost of goods sold.

Retail businesses purchase the items that are sold in their stores or online from manufacturers and wholesalers. For retail businesses, cost of goods sold represents the cost of purchasing these items from the manufacturer or wholesaler.

For instance, in our Bonnie's Beachwear example, the store purchases the bathing suits and other beachwear it sells at an average price of $18 and later resells these items at a higher price.

Manufacturing businesses purchase raw materials, and use the labor and machinery in their factories to create the products they then sell to wholesalers or retailers. For manufacturing businesses, cost of goods sold represents the expense of purchasing the raw materials, plus the cost of the labor and machine time needed to turn the raw materials into finished products.

Using our Boutique Handbags example: In order to manufacture the handbags it sells to retailers, the company would first have to purchase the raw materials for the handbags (such as fabric, hinges and clasps), and then use its workers and machines to convert the raw materials into finished handbags.

Cost of goods sold is often referred to as a variable expense. That is, the cost of goods sold expense will vary depending on the business's level of sales. If the company is doing well and has lots of sales, the cost of goods sold will be higher (since the business has to buy more items for resale or manufacture more items) than if the business isn't making as many sales.

BY ANY OTHER NAME

Cost of goods sold on the profit and loss statement can also be called *COGS*, and you'll find cost of services sometimes referred as *COS*.

Cost of Services

If you own a service business, costs of goods sold gets changed to cost of services on the profit and loss statement.

The primary product a service sells is the labor of its owners and employees. The cost of services represents the expense of providing these services. In other words, it's the cost of the salaries of the owners and employees when they provide the services of the business.

In our example of Uptown Chiropractic, the patient services are provided by Dr. Press, who owns the business, as well as by two chiropractic assistants. When preparing the profit and loss statement, the accountants will need to make some judgment calls about whether the salaries of Dr. Press and his chiropractic assistants should be called a cost of services for the business or an operating expense.

In most instances, the full salaries of the chiropractic assistants will be classified as a cost of services since these workers are engaged in patient treatment.

As the owner of the business, Dr. Press will spend some of his time treating patients and the remainder of his time administering and marketing the business. This presents a dilemma for his accountants. In preparing the profit and loss statement, they'll probably ask Dr. Press to estimate how much time he spends working in each area. Under accounting rules, the accountants may chose to allocate a percentage of Dr. Press' salary as an operating expense and the remainder to cost of services, or they may chose to allocate his full salary as a cost of services. Once again, as we stated in the "Profit Is an Estimate" section, the accountants are forced to estimate cost of services and estimate operating expenses.

Cost of services can be found on the profit and loss statement for many service businesses, including consultancies, law firms, advertising agencies, public relations firms, and even accounting firms. For instance, in a consulting business, the primary expenses are the consultant's salaries, and you'll typically find them listed as a cost of services on the profit and loss statement. Some service businesses may have both cost of goods sold and cost of services. For instance, when you take your car to the garage for repairs, the bill is generally broken out into two sections: the parts used in the repair of the car and a labor charge for the mechanic who worked on the car. The labor charge for the mechanic is a cost of services for the garage, and the purchase costs of the parts are a costs of goods sold.

Gross Profit

The difference between a business's revenue and the cost of goods sold or cost of services is known as the gross profit. Gross profit measures how much money a business makes on each sale.

A business's gross profit represents the money that's available to pay the operating expenses. For a manufacturing or retail business, the gross profit is the average profit the company makes on the sale of each item. For a service business, the gross profit is the average profit the firm makes on each service provided.

Below, there are two examples of how gross profit might be shown on a profit and loss statement for a retail business and a service business.

Gross Profit for a Retail Business

Sales Activities	
Revenue	$100,000
Cost of Goods Sold	$36,000
Gross Profit	**$64,000**

Gross Profit for a Service Business

Sales Activities	
Revenue	$25,000
Cost of Goods Sold	$10,000
Gross Profit	**$15,000**

Operating Expenses

Remember, there are two types of primary expenses that businesses incur: cost of goods sold and operating expenses. We discussed cost of goods sold earlier, so let's tackle operating expenses here.

In addition to the costs of providing services or the purchasing or manufacturing of products to be sold to customers, all companies have ongoing expenses that must be paid each month regardless of the number of sales the business makes. These are the business's operating expenses.

Operating expenses are typically grouped into three categories: selling, research and development, and general and administrative.

Selling Expenses

The costs of advertising, marketing and selling the business's goods or services come under selling expenses. Also included in this category are the costs of sales staff salaries as well as expenses for purchasing advertisements in newspapers or on the web. This category might also include the cost of outside services, such as graphic or web designers who help create the business's marketing materials or run its e-commerce site.

Research and Development Expenses

Manufacturing and high-tech businesses often spend money on research and development to develop new products for the business. Research and development expenses are treated as an operating expense since they're typically not directly related to the sale of existing goods and services.

General and Administrative Expenses

This category includes such expenses as rent and utilities payments that allow the business to keep its doors open. It also includes the costs of paying the salaries of the staff devoted to managing and administering the business, including the company president, accountants, and the receptionist.

Finally, monthly payments on any equipment leases would also be classified as general and administrative expenses. For instance, in our Uptown Chiropractic example, the business leases most of the treatment equipment used in its offices rather than purchasing it, and the payments on these leases would be accounted for as a general and administrative expense.

BY ANY OTHER NAME

You'll see research and development also called *R&D* on a profit and loss statement, and general and administrative expenses listed as *G&A*. At times, selling expenses are grouped with general and administrative and called *SGA*.

Depreciation

There is one additional type of operating expense that any business that owns equipment or machinery will have: depreciation. Depreciation allows a business to deduct the periodic wear and tear on equipment and machinery as an expense on the profit and loss statement.

The concept of depreciation is that assets of the business—equipment, machinery, and even real estate—will lose value as they wear out over time from use, and the business should be allowed to recognize this loss of value as an expense of operating the business.

Depreciation is what's known as a "noncash expense." That is, depreciation is an accounting event only. As the asset loses value, the business doesn't make any cash payments but is allowed to report a reduced operating profit. Although no cash changes hands, the reduced operating profit means the business will have a smaller tax liability. Let's look at several examples of assets that might be depreciated:

Consider a construction company that purchases a dump truck for use in its business. The dump truck is used to haul dirt and gravel to and from construction sites on a daily basis. Each time the truck is used, it wears out a little bit. As it's used, its value declines. Over the course of five years or so, the truck wears out, and its value falls to zero. If the truck cost $50,000 to purchase, and it lost $10,000 of value each year from use, a depreciation expense allows the business to recognize this $10,000 loss of value each year as an operating expense on its profit and loss statement.

A similar example would be a personal computer and software purchased for use by a business. Over time, the value of the computer and the software declines due to technological obsolescence. Over the course of a few years, the computer and software become obsolete and will need to be replaced. A depreciation expense allows the business to recognize this decline on its profit and loss statement.

In our sample companies, our manufacturer, Boutique Handbags, will depreciate the handbag-manufacturing equipment; our retail business, Bonnie's Beachwear, will depreciate the furniture and fixtures it has purchased to outfit the store; and our service business, Uptown Chiropractic, will be able to depreciate the computers and other equipment it has purchased for use in the office. Uptown Chiropractic will not, however, be able to depreciate its treatment equipment because it's leasing this equipment and doesn't own it.

Operating Profit

When you deduct operating expenses from gross profit, you get operating profit—the profit from the operations of the business.

This is the profit the business earns by selling its goods and services, paying for those goods and services, and paying all the other business operating expenses.

Let's expand our profit and loss statement to include a breakout of operating expenses (see page 59).

Typical Profit and Loss Statement
Operating Profit

Sales Activities	
Revenue	$100,000
Cost of Goods Sold	$36,000
Gross Profit	**$64,000**
Operating Expenses	
Selling Expenses	$15,000
Research and Development	$4,000
General and Administrative	$20,000
Depreciation	$5,000
Operating Profit	**$20,000**

BY ANY OTHER NAME

Operating profit goes by a variety of names. It's often referred to as *earnings before interest and taxes (EBIT)*, since interest and taxes aren't deducted prior to calculating operating profit. You'll also see operating profit called *operating income* or *income from operations*.

Interest

Although a business that borrows money must make an interest payment on the loan each month, interest payments aren't considered operating expenses under accounting rules. As a result, interest payments appear on a profit and loss statement on a separate line below operating profit.

Why is interest not considered an operating expense? The answer naturally lies in accounting and an accountant's view of financial statements.

One of the purposes of financial statements is to allow the comparison of one company to another, or one industry to another. Accountants view borrowing by a company to be an individual decision. One company might borrow to purchase a piece of equipment while another might pay for the purchase using cash from operations. If you were to compare the operating profit from the company that borrowed (and was paying interest) with the operating profit from the company that didn't borrow (and wasn't paying interest), you might not get an apples-to-apples comparison. Therefore, the accounting rules say to include interest as a separate item on the profit and loss statement.

One final note about loans and the profit and loss statement: Only the interest on the loan is treated as an expense. The repayment of the principal isn't an expense item because the business is considered to be returning the money it borrowed. The loan proceeds weren't considered revenue when they were received, and they're not considered an expense when they're repaid.

Profit Before Taxes

Profit before taxes is determined by subtracting any interest payments from the operating profit. Profit before taxes is the profit on which the business will be taxed. (An example of a profit and loss statement after including interest payments and calculating profit before taxes is shown on page 61.)

BY ANY OTHER NAME

Profit before taxes is also known as *earnings before taxes (or EBT)* and *income before taxes.*

Typical Profit and Loss Statement
Profit Before Taxes

Sales Activities	
Revenue	$100,000
Cost of Goods Sold	$36,000
Gross Profit	**$64,000**
Operating Expenses	
Selling Expenses	$15,000
Research and Development	$4,000
General and Administrative	$20,000
Depreciation	$5,000
Operating Profit	**$20,000**
Interest	$4,000
Profit Before Taxes	**$16,000**

Income Taxes

The next item on the profit and loss statement is the taxes paid on the profits of the business. Presently in the United States, the federal government taxes business profits at a rate of 35 percent. Additionally, many states also impose a tax on corporate profits that can be as high as 10 percent.

Net Profit

The final line on the profit and loss statement is net profit. Net profit is determined by subtracting federal and state income taxes from profit before taxes.

If net profit is positive, the business made money. If net profit is negative, the business lost money.

BY ANY OTHER NAME

The net profit line on a profit and loss statement is often referred to as the business's *net income*, and many times as the *bottom line* since it's the last line on the profit and loss statement. When a manager or business owner wants to know what's the bottom line, he's asking about the net profit.

You'll see the net profit line on our final table for this chapter, which presents a complete profit and loss statement (below).

Complete Profit and Loss Statement

Sales Activities	
Revenue	$100,000
Cost of Goods Sold	$36,000
Gross Profit	**$64,000**
Operating Expenses	
Selling Expenses	$15,000
Research and Development	$4,000
General and Administrative	$20,000
Depreciation	$5,000
Operating Profit	**$20,000**
Interest	$4,000
Profit Before Taxes	**$16,000**
Income Taxes	$5,600
Net Profit	**$10,400**

Now let's take a look at the development of a profit and loss statement for one of our sample businesses.

Bonnie's Beachwear Profit and Loss Statement

We again use Bonnie's Beachwear as our sample company to examine a monthly profit and loss statement. Remember, Bonnie's Beachwear generates revenue by selling bathing suits, coverups and casual beachwear from its retail store in a busy shopping district across from Miami's South Beach.

Sale Activities

Bonnie's Beachwear makes money by purchasing inventory for an average price of $18 and reselling it for an average price of $50. The business accepts cash, checks, and credit cards from its customers for purchases. When the business accepts a check, it can take anywhere from three days to a week for the check to clear the bank. When it accepts a credit card, it may take several days for the credit card processing company to electronically transfer the funds to the business's bank account. In other words, when Bonnie's makes a sale, it may be a few days or a week before the business receives the cash for the sale.

However, as a retail business, under the rules of accrual accounting, Bonnie's Beachwear is required to recognize the revenue from a sale when the sale occurs, regardless of when the store actually receives the cash. That is, the sale occurs when the customer purchases the merchandise at the cash register rather than when the business actually gets the cash. If Bonnie's sold 1,000 items during the month at an average price of $50, the business would have revenue of $50,000 on its profit and loss statement for the month.

As a retail business, under the rules of accrual accounting, Bonnie's Beachwear is also required to recognize the cost of the products sold on its profit and loss statement at the time of the sale. This would be when the customer purchases the merchandise at the cash register.

Like any retail business, before Bonnie's can sell any products, it first must acquire them from a manufacturer or wholesaler. These products become part of Bonnie's inventory and are placed on the shelves and display racks of the store so they're available for purchase by customers.

When a retailer purchases products for resale from a manufacturer or wholesaler, it's typically allowed a specified period, such as 30 or 60 days, before it's required to pay for the products. In many instances, the retailer will be able to sell the products before it pays for them. In other instances, it may not sell the products right away and will have to pay suppliers for products that are still on the shelves.

GROSS PROFIT measures how much money a business makes on each sale.

Under accounting rules, the cost of the products Bonnie's sells get recognized on the profit and loss statement at the time of sale— when the customer purchases the merchandise at the cash register. The business can't recognize the cost of the products on its profit and loss statement when they're acquired from the manufacturer or wholesaler or when they're placed in the store's inventory. Even if 30 days has passed and the business has paid the manufacturer or wholesaler for the products, cost of goods sold only gets recognized when the customer purchases the product at the cash register.

If Bonnie's sold 1,000 items during the month at an average cost of $18, the business would have a cost of goods sold of $18,000 on the profit and loss statement. Even if Bonnie's purchased or paid for additional inventory during the month, the cost of goods sold should include only the merchandise actually sold during the month.

Gross Profit

As you'll recall, the gross profit of the business is revenue less cost of goods sold. If Bonnie's had revenue of $50,000 for the month, and cost of goods sold of $18,000, the gross profit for the business would be $32,000 for the month ($50,000 - $18,000 = $32,000).

The table below shows the sale activities section of Bonnie's monthly profit and loss statement.

Bonnie's Beachwear Profit and Loss Statement
Gross Profit

Sales Activities	
Revenue	$50,000
Cost of Goods Sold	$18,000
Gross Profit	**$32,000**

Operating Expenses

Chapter 3 presented a sample cash flow statement for Bonnie's Beachwear, where we indicated that the business paid $22,000 each month in operating expenses.

The "Monthly Cash Payments" chart on page 38 in Chapter 3 shows a breakdown of Bonnie's $22,000 in cash operating expenses:

- *Rent:* $3,000
- *Utilities:* $1,500
- *Sales staff salaries:* $10,000
- *Owner's salary:* $4,500
- *Advertising:* $2,000
- *Accounting, payroll and legal:* $1,000

After reviewing these expenses, we see that Bonnie's Beachwear doesn't have any research and development expenses. This would be typical, since as a small retail business, Bonnie's is only selling products designed and developed by others, and isn't designing or developing its own products.

The operating expenses of Bonnie's Beachwear can be grouped into either selling expenses or general and administrative. The two primary selling expenses are the $2,000 per month advertising costs and the $10,000 per month sales staff salaries. Rent ($3,000), utilities ($1,500), and accounting, payroll and legal services ($1,000) are general and administrative expenses.

When you deduct OPERATING EXPENSES from gross profit, you get OPERATING PROFIT.

But how should the $4,500 per month owner's salary be treated? Is this a selling or a general and administrative expense? Recall from our discussion in the "Cost of Goods Sold" section above, that sometimes it's necessary for an accountant to estimate how a particular expense should be allocated. For instance, the accountant had to estimate how much time Dr. Press spent administering the chiropractic business and how much time he spent treating patients.

It is the same decision here. The accountant would have to estimate how much of Bonnie's time is spent managing and administering the business, and how much time is spent on the sales floor selling to customers. Given that the business has a dedicated sales staff, the accountant might decide to allocate all the owner's time as general and administrative, and none of it as a selling expense.

In addition to the selling and general and administrative expenses, Bonnie's Beachwear should recognize a depreciation expense. Recall from Chapter 2 that the business spent $40,000 to purchase furniture and fixtures to outfit the sales area of the store and an additional $10,000 on computerized cash registers and inventory management software.

The furniture, fixtures and equipment that Bonnie's purchased became assets of the business that must be depreciated. Each month, a portion of the $50,000 total purchase cost should be recognized as an operating expense on the profit and loss statement. Assuming these assets are depreciated over five years, the annual depreciation would be $10,000. Dividing the annual depreciation by 12 produces a monthly depreciation of $833.

Operating Profit

The business's monthly operating profit is determined by subtracting the sum of the operating expenses ($22,833) from the gross profit ($32,000 - $22,833 = $9,167). The chart below shows the monthly operating profit for Bonnie's Beachwear.

Bonnie's Beachwear Profit and Loss Statement
Operating Profit

Sales Activities	
Revenue	$50,000
Cost of Goods Sold	$18,000
Gross Profit	**$32,000**
Operating Expenses	
Selling Expenses	
Advertising	$2,000
Sales Staff Salary	$10,000
General and Administrative	
Rent	$3,000
Utilities	$1,500
Owner's Salary	$4,500
Accounting, Payroll and Legal	$1,000
Depreciation	$833
Operating Profit	**$9,167**

Interest

As you can see from the description in Chapter 2 and the discussion above, a business owner can incur significant costs in starting a business. Often, it will cost more to start a business than the owner has available in personal funds. When this happens, the business must borrow the rest of the money it needs.

When that happens, the business must pay interest on the money borrowed. This interest is deducted from operating profit on the profit and loss statement. For our sample profit and loss statement, let's assume that Bonnie's Beachwear must pay $750 per month in interest.

Profit Before Taxes

If we subtract the interest payment from the operating profit, we have profit before taxes. In our sample profit and loss statement on page 69, the profit before taxes for Bonnie's Beachwear was $8,417 ($9,167 - $750 = $8,417).

Bonnie's Beachwear Profit and Loss Statement
Profit Before Taxes

Sales Activities	
Revenue	$50,000
Cost of Goods Sold	$18,000
Gross Profit	**$32,000**
Operating Expenses	
Selling Expenses	
Advertising	$2,000
Sales Staff Salary	$10,000
General and Administrative	
Rent	$3,000
Utilities	$1,500
Owners' Salary	$4,500
Accounting, Payroll and Legal	$1,000
Depreciation	$833
Operating Profit	**$9,167**
Interest	$750
Profit Before Taxes	**$8,417**

Income Taxes

The good news is Bonnie's Beachwear is making a profit. We've deducted all cost of goods sold, operating expenses, and interest from revenue, and have a positive profit before taxes.

The bad news is, since the business is making a profit, it owes the government taxes on that profit.

As discussed in the "Income Taxes" section above, the current federal tax rate for businesses is 35 percent, and the store may owe the state a business income tax as well.

Using 35 percent as the tax rate (and ignoring the state tax rate for purposes of this example), Bonnie's Beachwear would owe

$2,946 (35% of its $8,417 profit before taxes) in income taxes to the federal government.

Net Profit

The bottom line on the profit and loss statement for Bonnie's Beachwear is net profit, which is determined by subtracting taxes from profit before taxes. In our example (below), Bonnie's Beachwear made a net profit of $5,471 ($8,417 - $2,946 = $5,471). This is the amount of profit the business made for the month on an accounting basis.

Bonnie's Beachwear Profit and Loss Statement
Profit After Taxes

Sales Activities	
Revenue	$50,000
Cost of Goods Sold	$18,000
Gross Profit	**$32,000**
Operating Expenses	
Selling Expenses	
Advertising	$2,000
Sales Staff Salary	$10,000
General and Administrative	
Rent	$3,000
Utilities	$1,500
Owners' Salary	$4,500
Accounting, Payroll and Legal	$1,000
Depreciation	$833
Operating Profit	**$9,167**
Interest	$750
Profit Before Taxes	**$8,417**
Income Taxes @ 35%	$2,946
Net Profit	**$5,471**

Chapter 3 presented a monthly cash flow statement for Bonnie's Beachwear. This chapter has presented a monthly profit and loss statement.

The next chapter discusses how a business's net profit can differ from the cash flow, and why a profitable business needs both.

CHAPTER SIX

The Difference Between Cash and Profit

 In the preceding chapters, we presented the cash flow statement and the profit and loss statement. In Chapter 3, we discussed how the cash flow statement shows the cash the business received during the month and the cash the business paid during the month. In Chapter 4, we identified three types of cash flow: operating cash flow, asset activity cash flow, and financing activity cash flow. And in the last chapter, we talked about how accounting rules can affect a profit and loss statement and the estimated and noncash nature of the items included on a profit and loss statement.

This chapter will discuss the difference between cash and profit, and why a profitable business needs both. Let's look at some of the reasons cash and profit may be different.

Asset and Financing Activity

The profit and loss statement primarily reflects the business's operating activity. Net profit is calculated as the business's revenue from selling goods or services less its expenses. That is, revenue less costs of goods sold (or cost of services provided) and operating expenses. Net profit results from the operation of the business.

If a company is engaged in asset activity or financing activity, the cash flow will differ from the profit of the business. For example, consider a manufacturing business that purchases a $10,000 machine to be used in the factory to produce products. Here's how the purchase gets reflected on the cash flow statement and the profit and loss statement:

- This $10,000 purchase will be classified as asset activity on the cash flow statement. As a result of spending $10,000 to purchase an asset, the business's cash outflows are increased by $10,000 and it has $10,000 less cash at the end of the month.

- The purchase adds $10,000 to the company's assets. (See Chapter 7 on the balance sheet for further discussion about assets.)

- Although the business's cash is reduced by $10,000, its profit is not reduced by $10,000 since the purchase is not an operating expense or a cost of goods sold.

- Instead, the business is allowed to include depreciation as an operating expense on the profit and loss statement to reflect the periodic wear and tear on the machine during the production process. On the monthly profit and loss statement, the depreciation for this $10,000 machine might be $200.

The net effect of this purchase is that the company has spent $10,000 of cash on an asset activity, but the business's profit is only reduced by the $200 in depreciation.

The purchase of this machine has an interesting long-term effect on the profit and loss statement of the business. If we look at the next month's cash flow statement, we'll see no effect from the purchase of the machine. The $10,000 was spent in a prior month, so it doesn't impact any of the succeeding month's cash flow. However, if we look at next month's profit and loss statement, we'll continue to see the $200 depreciation of the machine for the next several years. The profits of the business will be reduced by a noncash $200 depreciation expense each month until the machine is fully depreciated.

Timing

The difference between cash and profit can result from a timing difference between when the business recognizes revenue and expenses and when it receives or pays cash.

As we discussed in Chapter 5, under accounting rules, revenue is recognized by many businesses as occurring at the time of sale. However, the timing of the sale may occur before the business receives the cash for the sale.

The DIFFERENCES between cash and profit can result from a TIMING difference.

Consider a manufacturing company that records a sale when the customer places the order rather than when the customer pays for products, or a retail business that records a sale when the customer purchases the product at the cash register rather than when a check clears the bank or the retailer receives payment from the credit card company. The business may be recognizing the revenue from a sale on its profit and loss statement before it has received the cash.

The same is true of expenses. Expenses for cost of goods sold are recognized on the profit and loss statement at the time of sale. A retail business may have sold goods from its inventory, where it paid the manufacturer or wholesaler for the goods in a prior month, or it may have just received a shipment of the goods, for which it has not yet paid.

In either case, the cash payments may not occur in the same accounting period as the sale of the goods. When this happens, the profit and loss statement will differ from the cash flow statement.

Now that we've identified some reasons why cash and profit may be different, let's examine why a business needs both cash and profit.

Profit Without Cash

First, we'll discuss how a business can have profit without cash. Profit without cash generally results when a business recognizes revenues on its profit and loss statement before the cash from those revenues is received by the business. Profit without cash is most likely to occur when a business first starts out or when revenues are growing.

Consider what happens when our manufacturing company, Boutique Handbags, begins to grow. As we discussed in Chapter 2, Boutique Handbags manufactures higher-end women's handbags for resale to women's specialty stores and high-end department stores. The handbags cost $20 each to manufacture and are sold by Boutique for $40 each.

For the sake of our example, let's assume the business's operating expenses are $12,000 per month and that the operating expenses don't change as long as the volume is at or below 2,000 units per month.

As discussed above, one of the key differences between cash and profit is timing. When Boutique Handbags sells the handbags to the retailers, it allows the retailer 60 days to pay. Boutique Handbags receives cash for the products it sells 60 days after the sale, but it has to pay for the labor and materials at the time the handbags are manufactured.

Let's look at what happens to Boutique Handbags' profits as it begins operations, and production volume and sales revenue increases. The business sells 1,000 handbags in January, 1,250 handbags in February, and 1,500 handbags in March and April. The business recognizes the revenue from the sale of the handbags in the month in which they are sold. As the "Profit and Loss Statement" on page 77 shows, Boutique Handbags is profitable each month.

Boutique Handbags Profit and Loss Statement

	January	February	March	April
Sales Activities				
Revenue	$40,000	$50,000	$60,000	$60,000
Cost of Goods Sold	$20,000	$25,000	$30,000	$30,000
Gross Profit	**$20,000**	**$25,000**	**$30,000**	**$30,000**
Operating Expenses	$12,000	$12,000	$12,000	$12,000
Profit Before Taxes	**$8,000**	**$13,000**	**$18,000**	**$18,000**
Income Taxes	$2,800	$4,550	$6,300	$6,300
Net Profit	**$5,200**	**$8,450**	**$11,700**	**$11,700**
Cumulative Profit (Jan.–Mar.)		**$25,350**		

Now let's review the business's cash flow. Boutique Handbags' "Cash Flow Statement" for the same period is found below.

Boutique Handbags Cash Flow Statement

	January	February	March	April
Cash Generated from Operating Activities				
Collections of Accounts Receivable	$0	$0	$40,000	$50,000
Total Cash from Operating Activities	**$0**	**$0**	**$40,000**	**$50,000**
Cash Used in Operating Activities				
Handbag Manufacturing	$20,000	$25,000	$30,000	$30,000
Operating Expenses	$12,000	$12,000	$12,000	$12,000
Income Taxes	$2,800	$4,550	$6,300	$6,300
Total Cash Used in Operating Activities	**$34,800**	**$41,550**	**$48,300**	**$48,300**
Cash Flow	**($34,800)**	**($41,550)**	**($8,300)**	**$1,700**
Cumulative Cash Flow (Jan.–Mar.)		**($84,650)**		

The business's cash flow is negative in each of the first three months. Why does a business that showed profits on the profit and loss statement have negative cash flow during this growth period? The answer lies in the timing and the rules of accounting. On its profit and loss statement, Boutique Handbags recognizes the revenue from its sales in the month in which the sale occurred, yet it doesn't receive the cash until two months later. Let's look at the activity in each month.

January

On the accounting-based profit and loss statement, Boutique Handbags recognizes revenue of $40,000 for the sale of 1,000 handbags at $40 each, recognizes a cost of goods sold of $20,000 (1,000 handbags at a cost of $20 each), and incurs operating expenses of $12,000. The profit before taxes of the business is $8,000, and the net profit after taxes is $5,200.

Because of the timing difference between the recognition of the revenue on the profit and loss statement and the receipt of payment for the sale in 60 days, the company doesn't receive any cash payments for sales in January, and yet it must pay $20,000 in expenses to manufacture the handbags and $12,000 in operating expenses.

Additionally, because the business has generated an accounting profit in January based on the profit and loss statement, the business will owe taxes on this profit, even though the cash hasn't been received.

During January, the business is profitable, yet it spends $34,800 more in cash than it receives. In order for Boutique Handbags to pay its bills for January, it would have needed to begin the month with at least $34,800 in cash.

February

In February, the business increases its sales volume to 1,250 units, yet it still experiences the same situation as in January. The profit and loss statement shows a business that generated a profit before taxes of $13,000 and a net profit of $8,450, yet the cash flow statement shows it spent $41,550 more in cash than it took in during the month. Once again, for the business to pay its bills for February, it would have needed to begin the month with at least $41,550 in cash.

March

In March, Boutique Handbags increases its sales volume to 1,500 units, and the profit and loss statement shows a profitable business. Profit before taxes is $18,000 and net profit is $11,700.

The business finally begins to receive some cash, as the accounts receivable for the sales in January are paid. The business is paid $40,000 by its customers for the products it manufactured and sold in January.

Yet the cash flow of the business is still negative. This is a result of the sales volume increasing each month and the business paying $30,000 to manufacture 1,500 handbags in March, plus $12,000 in operating expenses, while only being paid $40,000 for the handbags it sold in January.

Overall, the business spends $8,300 more cash in March than it receives. The same scenario is repeated: For the business to pay its bills in March, it would have needed to begin the month with at least $8,300 in cash.

April

By April, sales have leveled off at 1,500 units per month, and the cash from sales made in February is collected. In April, for the first time, the business shows an accounting profit on the profit and loss statement as well as a positive cash flow on the cash flow statement.

In Review

In this section, we've presented an example of a business that's growing and has a timing difference between when revenue is recognized on the profit and loss statement and when cash is actually received.

These two factors lead to a situation where Boutique Handbags shows a net profit, and in fact is paying taxes on this profit, and yet has a significant negative cash flow.

For the business to begin operations, or even to increase its monthly sales volume, it will need to have some cash on hand at the start of each month so the bills can be paid while it waits for the payments from its customers to begin.

In our example, Boutique Handbags generated net profits of $25,350 during the first three months of operations, yet it had a cumulative negative cash flow of $84,650 during the same period. If the business didn't have this cash available, it wouldn't be able to pay its bills and would be in danger of failing. Clearly Boutique Handbags needs both profit and cash to survive.

This is a somewhat extreme example, but it's representative of the cash flow issues many businesses face as they begin operations or seek to expand.

Cash Without Profit

Now let's examine how a business can have cash without profit. Cash without profit generally occurs when a business is able to sell its products and receive payment for those products before paying the expenses of the business.

This is typical of many restaurants and retail establishments, where the customer pays cash at the time of purchase, and the business may be allowed 30 or 60 days to pay the manufacturer or wholesaler for the products that are sold.

Let's again use our retail business, Bonnie's Beachwear, as an example. As discussed in Chapter 2, Bonnie's Beachwear sells bathing suits and other beach attire from a store in Miami's South Beach neighborhood. The retail price of the average sale is $50, and the cost of goods for the average sale is $18.

For the purposes of this example, let's assume the business's monthly operating expenses are $22,000, which include the cost of rent, utilities, sales staff and owner's salaries, advertising, and other general and administrative expenses. Also assume that the cash payments are received at the time of sale and that the wholesaler that supplies the company with its beachwear inventory allows Bonnie's to pay in 30 days.

Let's look at what happens as Bonnie's Beachwear begins operations. A "Profit and Loss Statement" for Bonnie's Beachwear is presented below. Bonnie's opens its doors on June 1 and is immediately successful, selling 500 bathing suits in June, 650 bathing suits in July, 680 bathing suits in August, and 700 bathing suits in September. However, the net profit is negative during the first three months of operation. The business lost money in June, July and August.

Bonnie's Beachwear Profit and Loss Statement

	June	July	August	September
Sales Activities				
Revenue	$25,000	$32,500	$34,000	$35,000
Cost of Goods Sold	$9,000	$11,700	$12,240	$12,600
Gross Profit	**$16,000**	**$20,800**	**$21,760**	**$22,400**
Operating Expenses	$22,000	$22,000	$22,000	$22,000
Profit Before Taxes	**($6,000)**	**($1,200)**	**($240)**	**$400**
Income Taxes	$0	$0	$0	$140
Net Profit	**($6,000)**	**($1,200)**	**($240)**	**$260**
Cumulative Profit (Jun.–Aug.)		**($7,440)**		

Bonnie's Beachwear's "Cash Flow Statement" below represents the same period. The cash flow statement shows a positive cash flow for each month. That is, the business is generating more cash from operations than it's spending. How can a business that's not making a profit have a positive cash flow from operations?

Bonnie's Beachwear Cash Flow Statement

	June	July	August	September
Cash Generated from				
Operating Activities				
Cash Receipts from Sales	$25,000	$32,500	$34,000	$35,000
Total Cash from				
Operating Activities	**$25,000**	**$32,500**	**$34,000**	**$35,000**
Cash Used in Operating				
Activities				
Payment of Accounts				
Payable	$0	$9,000	$11,700	$12,240
Operating Expenses	$22,000	$22,000	$22,000	$22,000
Income Taxes	$0	$0	$0	$140
Total Cash Used in				
Operating Activities	**$22,000**	**$31,000**	**$33,700**	**$34,380**
Cash Flow	**$3,000**	**$1,500**	**$300**	**$620**
Cumulative Cash Flow (Jun.–Aug.)		**$4,800**		

The answer again lies in the timing of the cash flows and the rules of accounting. The profit and loss statement for Bonnie's Beachwear recognizes revenue and cost of goods sold at the time the customer purchases the beachwear. When the cost of goods sold and operating expenses are subtracted from revenue, the resulting net profit is negative. On an accounting basis, the business has lost money.

The business is losing money during these first three months because it doesn't have sufficient revenue. It's not selling enough beachwear to cover its costs of goods sold and to pay the business's operating expenses.

However, the cash flow statement presents a different picture. Because Bonnie's Beachwear has 30 days to pay the wholesaler for the beachwear it sells—and its business is growing—the cash flow statement shows a positive picture of the business. The cash flow is positive because it doesn't include payment to suppliers for the inventory.

Let's look at this activity for each month.

June

On the accounting-based profit and loss statement for June, Bonnie's Beachwear recognizes revenue of $25,000 for the sale of 500 bathing suits and beach accessories at an average price of $50, records a cost of goods sold of $9,000 for the 500 bathing suits and beach accessories sold (500 units sold at an average cost of $18), and incurs operating expenses of $22,000. The profit before taxes is negative, as is the net profit, indicating a loss for the month. Because the profit before taxes is negative, the business doesn't owe any taxes.

The cash flow statement differs from the profit and loss statement due to the timing of payments for products the business sells. Remember, Bonnie's can take 30 days to pay the wholesaler for the products it sells. The cash flow statement for June shows cash received from sales of $25,000 and operating expenses of $22,000, but no payment for the purchase of the products it resold. During the month, the business receives $3,000 more in cash than it spends. The business does owe $9,000 for the merchandise it sells, but the bills for these products aren't due yet, so the cash flow looks good.

July

In July, Bonnie's Beachwear increases its sales volume to 650 items, generating revenue of $32,500. Once again, the net profit of the business is negative, and the business generates more cash than it spends.

Even though the business sells 650 items during the month, the cost of goods sold and operating expenses still exceed revenue, and the profit and loss statement shows the business losing money.

On the cash flow statement, we see that Bonnie's Beachwear received $32,500 in revenue for the sale of 650 items and paid $22,000 in operating expenses, as well as $9,000 in accounts payable to the wholesaler for the merchandise it sold in June.

Because sales grew during the month, the business generated additional revenue and was able to pay the previous month's bills to the wholesalers, and end the month with a positive cash flow.

August

In August, Bonnie's Beachwear increases its sales volume to 680 units, generating revenue of $34,000. As in June and July, the net profit is negative. The $34,000 in revenue is slightly less than the cost of goods sold and operating expenses for the month. The business is still not selling enough merchandise to cover its cost of goods sold and operating expenses

However, once again the business has a positive cash flow for the month. As in July, this is due to the additional revenue from an increase in sales and the fact that the business is paying the wholesaler for merchandise purchased in a prior month when the sales volume was smaller.

September

It's not until September, when the sales volume increases to 700 units, that Bonnie's Beachwear generates a positive net profit and a positive cash flow.

In Review

In this section, we've presented an example of a business that's growing, isn't selling a sufficient number of units each month to generate a profit, and yet has a positive cash flow. This is the result of a difference between when revenue and expenses are recognized on the profit and loss statement and when the expenses of the business are paid.

During the first three months of operation, Bonnie's Beachwear had a net loss of $7,440, yet had a positive cash flow of $4,800. It's very important to note that if Bonnie had only looked at the cash flow statement, seen the positive cash flow, and withdrawn the $4,800 from the business, when sales leveled off or declined, the business wouldn't have sufficient cash to pay the wholesaler for the merchandise it sold.

A business may show a POSITIVE cash flow, and yet may be unprofitable.

The example we've presented here is typical of many companies as they grow. Due to the timing difference between when revenue is received and the payment of expenses, a business may show a positive cash flow, and yet may be unprofitable.

As a business matures, the sales growth slows and sales volume tends to be more consistent period to period. When this happens, the revenue and expenses recognized on the profit and loss statement become more closely aligned with the revenue received and expenses paid on the cash flow statement.

If a business continues to be unprofitable, it will eventually run out of cash as prior-period bills come due.

CHAPTER SEVEN

Balance Sheet Basics

Now that we've covered the cash flow statement and the profit and loss statement, let's look at the last of the primary financial statements—the balance sheet. The role of the balance sheet is to provide a financial snapshot of a business at a given point.

Understanding the Balance Sheet

Before we examine the sections of the balance sheet in detail, let's discuss the basic principles at work in this financial statement.

Simply put, the balance sheet shows a business's assets, liabilities and owners' equity. A business's assets are the things it owns, such as cash, money owed from customers and equipment. A business's liabilities are the debts it owes, and the owners' equity is the money the owners have invested in the business and the profits that haven't been distributed to the owners.

When a business acquires an asset, it must in some way pay for that asset. When the business pays, it either uses money it borrowed (a liability), or it uses money that belongs to the owners (owners' equity). Hence, the key concept of a balance sheet is that assets equal liabilities, plus owners' equity:

Assets = Liabilities + Owners' Equity

It is called a balance sheet because both sides of the equation are equal, or in balance.

The balance sheet shows the assets the business owns, as well as the source of the funds used to acquire those assets, either borrowed money or the owners' money. Since all assets are acquired using either borrowed money or the owners' money, the total of all assets must equal the total of all borrowed money, plus the owners' money. The "Balance Sheet Summary" below shows this equation in its most basic form. Of course, the balance sheet can get much more detailed, as you'll see later in the chapter.

Balance Sheet Summary	
Assets	$100,000
Total Assets	**$100,000**
Liabilities	$60,000
Owners Equity	$40,000
Total Liabilities and Owners' Equity	**$100,000**

A Snapshot

Like the profit and loss statement, the balance sheet is also an accounting statement, developed by your accountants (or your accounting software), using the rules of accounting. The profit and loss statement and the cash flow statement each reflect the operating activity of the company over a period of time, such as a month or year.

The balance sheet, on the other hand, is a snapshot of the business at a specific point in time such as the end of the month or the end of the year. The balance sheet summarizes the company's assets, liabilities and owners' equity as of a particular date.

Additionally, the entries on a balance sheet are carried at historical values. That is, it shows the asset's value at the time it was acquired. This is important because accountants look at how much an asset costs to acquire rather than how much it might be worth when the snapshot is taken. We'll discuss this further in the "Depreciation" section.

BY ANY OTHER NAME

Unlike the profit and loss statement, which goes by many names, the balance sheet is almost always referred to as the balance sheet. The only alternative name is the *statement of assets and liabilities*, which isn't commonly used.

Examining the Balance Sheet

Let's examine the contents of the balance sheet by taking a look at what's included in each section. Like the profit and loss statement, we'll be building the balance sheet as we progress through the chapter. We'll start by looking at the asset side of the balance sheet. Next, we'll explore the liabilities side of the balance sheet, and finally, the owners' equity section.

Assets

The assets section of the balance sheet includes the assets the business owns, such as cash, inventory, equipment, and any real estate or other buildings. The assets section is typically divided into two sections: current assets, and plant, property and equipment assets.

Current Assets

The current assets section of the balance sheet (see page 91) includes assets that are already in cash, or that the business can expect to convert to cash within one year. Current assets typically include:

- *Cash:* This includes the cash the business has on hand, in the cash draw, in the safe, or in one of the company's bank or credit union accounts. The cash balance at the end of the month on the balance sheet should be the same as the cash at the end of the month on the cash flow statement.

- *Accounts receivable:* The money that customers owe the business is called accounts receivable. For instance, our sample company Boutique Handbags sold its handbags to retailers but didn't expect to be paid for the handbags for 60 days. During these 60 days, the money owed by customers to Boutique Handbags is an accounts receivable of the business.

- *Inventory:* This includes merchandise received from manufacturers and suppliers that hasn't yet been sold to customers. For example, our retail store, Bonnie's Beachwear, needs to purchase inventory to stock the store before it can begin selling to customers.

- *Raw materials:* This includes materials purchased by the business to be used in the production process but that haven't yet been turned into products. Raw material assets are typically found in manufacturing businesses. For instance, our manufacturing business, Boutique Handbags, might include raw materials on its balance sheet to reflect the fabric and other material it purchases to use in the production of its handbags.

- *Work in process:* This reflects the value of goods currently in the production process. A work in process asset is often found on the balance sheets of large or specialized manufacturers. For example, an airplane might take several months to build, and the value of the airplane as it moves through the manufacturing process would be accounted for as work in process on the balance sheet.

Inventory, raw materials and work in process are generally included as current assets because they are typically expected to be brought through the production process and sold to customers within a year.

BY ANY OTHER NAME

Current assets are also known as *short-term* or *liquid assets*.

The current assets section of a typical balance sheet is shown below.

Typical Balance Sheet
Current Assets

Assets

Current Assets

Cash	$10,000
Accounts Receivable	$30,000
Inventory	$10,000
Raw Materials	$5,000
Work in Process	$5,000
Total Current Assets	**$60,000**

The assets section of the balance sheet might also include an item called prepaid expenses. The most common type of prepaid expenses are premiums on insurance policies. For instance, a business might pay in advance for insurance coverage for the next 12 months. Under accounting rules, since the business could receive a pro-rata refund of its premiums if it cancelled the policy before the end of 12 months, the amount that could be refunded is considered an asset of the business and reflected as a prepaid expense on the balance sheet. Accountants tend to include prepaid expenses on the balance sheet, even though for most businesses they are very small amounts.

Plant, Property and Equipment

Plant, property and equipment are assets used in the business's production and operating processes.

This category includes the equipment the company has purchased, the machinery in the factory, and any real estate the business owns. Plant, property and equipment also includes the furniture and fixtures a business owns as well as computers and software.

Most BUSINESSES have some plant, property and equipment assets.

Most businesses have some plant, property and equipment assets. Plant, property and equipment is very common for manufacturing businesses, but retail companies and service firms also purchase some assets that are used in the business processes, such as office furniture or the display racks in a retail store. Even consulting businesses have plant, property and equipment assets. For instance, the computer on which this chapter is being written is an equipment asset of the author's business.

Our manufacturing company, Boutique Handbags, purchased several pieces of cutting and sewing equipment that it uses in the manufacture of its handbags. Each of our sample companies purchased computer equipment and software that are used in the operation of the business.

Page 95 presents an example of what the plant, property and equipment section would like on a typical balance sheet.

BY ANY OTHER NAME

Plant, property and equipment assets are also referred to as *long-term assets*, *other assets* and *fixed assets* on the balance sheet.

Depreciation

Under accounting rules, plant, property and equipment assets are carried on the balance sheet at historical cost, which means the cost at which the asset was acquired. The current market value of the asset may be more or less than the historical cost, but the balance sheet will only reflect the historical cost.

How does the balance sheet reflect the fact that the value of an asset may be more or less than historical cost? Under accounting rules, if the value of the asset has increased, there's typically no adjustment to its value. Accountants want the asset kept at the lower historical cost value. This rule particularly affects companies which own real estate that has appreciated in value.

But many companies also own machinery and equipment that lose value as they wear out or become technologically obsolete. How is this decline in value reflected on the balance sheet? Accountants use depreciation to reflect that in fact many productive assets decline in value over time.

As discussed in Chapter 5, depreciation is a noncash operating expense that allows a business to deduct the periodic wear and tear on its equipment and machinery.

When the business depreciates an asset on its profit and loss statement, it also deducts the amount of depreciation from the asset's value on the balance sheet.

Because the balance sheet contains historical values, the depreciation entry on the balance sheet includes all the depreciation to-date for each plant, property and equipment asset. Each period the amount of depreciation increases, and the value of the asset less this accumulated depreciation decreases.

Let's look back at the depreciation example from Chapter 5. A construction company purchases a dump truck to use in its business for $50,000, the truck is expected to wear out over five years, and the business recognizes a depreciation expense of $10,000 each year for five years. The "Annual Depreciation" example below shows how the depreciation for this dump truck might appear on the business's balance sheet.

Typical Balance Sheet
Annual Depreciation Example

	2008	2009	2010
Plant, Property and Equipment			
Equipment (Dump Truck)	$50,000	$50,000	$50,000
Less: Accumulated Depreciation	($10,000)	($20,000)	($30,000)
Total Plant, Property and Equipment	**$40,000**	**$30,000**	**$20,000**

During the first year of ownership, the business depreciates the dump truck by $10,000. The balance sheet shows the original purchase cost of $50,000, the $10,000 in depreciation, and $40,000 as the remaining value of the truck in plant, property and equipment.

During the second year of ownership, the business depreciates the dump truck by an additional $10,000 to reflect the wear and tear on the truck during this year. The balance sheet continues to show the original purchase cost of $50,000 but now shows accumulated depreciation of $20,000 ($10,000 depreciation in each of the first two years), and $30,000 as the remaining value of the truck in plant, property and equipment.

During the third year, the dump truck is depreciated an additional $10,000, accumulated depreciation is now $30,000, and the net value of the truck on the balance sheet is $20,000. At the end of five years, the truck would be fully depreciated, and the value of the truck would be zero in the plant, property and equipment section of the balance sheet.

After five years, the truck might still be running well and be used by the business, but it would be fully depreciated and have a zero value on the balance sheet.

Typical Balance Sheet
Plant, Property and Equipment

Assets

Current Assets

Cash	$10,000
Accounts Receivable	$30,000
Inventory	$10,000
Raw Materials	$5,000
Work in Process	$5,000
Total Current Assets	**$60,000**

Plant, Property and Equipment

Equipment	$50,000
Less: Accumulated Depreciation	($10,000)
Total Plant, Property and Equipment	**$40,000**
Total Assets	**$100,000**

DEPRECIATION FAQS

Determining the appropriate amount of asset depreciation can be a complex and confusing process. One of the key uses of depreciation is to reduce a business's taxable income. Since depreciation reduces a business's taxable income, taxing agencies such as the IRS have developed some complex rules governing what assets can be depreciated, how depreciation can be calculated on these assets, and what the useful, or depreciable, life of an asset is. The IRS sets the rules of depreciation, and your accountant or your accounting software calculates the appropriate amount of depreciation.

Here are some FAQs about depreciation:

- *What can be depreciated?* In general, any asset the business purchases that is expected to have a useful life of more than one year should be depreciated. Using this rule, a business would depreciate a computer or software but wouldn't need to depreciate pencils, pens and other office supplies.

- *What's an asset's useful life?* To depreciate an asset, you first have to determine its depreciable, or useful, life. As with many things related to financial statements and taxes, there are rules that define an asset's useful life.

  Under IRS rules, the useful life of an asset can range from as few as three years to as many as 50 years. The chart on the following page shows the useful life for common types of business assets.

- *How is depreciation calculated?* There are several different ways to calculate depreciation. The simplest method of depreciation is known as straight-line depreciation. If a business uses straight-line depreciation, it will depreciate an asset by the same amount each year of the asset's useful life. For instance, if an asset cost $5,000, and its useful life is five years, the depreciation would be $1,000 per year for five years.

Throughout this book, we've calculated depreciation using the straight-line method in our discussions and in our examples. It's the most straightforward method and the easiest to explain.

Useful Life for Depreciation

Useful Life	Type of Asset
5 years	Trucks, automobiles, computers and peripherals, most industrial equipment
7 years	Office furniture and equipment, any unclassified assets
10 years	Property improvements, water transportation equipment, single-purpose agricultural buildings
20 years	Farm buildings, infrastructure
27.5 years	Real estate

The more complicated methods of calculating depreciation are known as accelerated depreciation. With accelerated depreciation, a business is able to depreciate more of an asset's value in the early years of use and less in the later years. This is similar to what might happen when you purchase a new car. The car loses more value in the first year than it does in the second year, and then loses more value in the second year than it does in the third year. There are several formulas for accelerated depreciation, such as "modified accelerated cost recovery system" (MACRS), "sum of the year's digits" (SOYD), or "double declining balance" (DDB), which are beyond the scope of this book. However, you may hear about these methods from your accountant.

Finally, there's a special section of the tax code in the United States pertaining to depreciation, known as Section 179. Section 179 allows a business to depreciate the entire value of an asset in the year of purchase. Section 179 is often used by small businesses to depreciate things like computers, software, and office and restaurant equipment.

A Word of Caution

This discussion isn't meant to be an all-encompassing description of depreciation. Depreciation is much too complicated to be covered in just a few paragraphs. This section is only meant to introduce the concept of depreciation and make you aware of how it can affect the financial statements and profitability of your business. The IRS has published entire manuals on depreciation, and a good accountant will be familiar with the depreciation alternatives. Additionally, tax and accounting software such as QuickBooks or TurboTax often are useful in managing depreciation.

The key is to understand that there are multiple depreciation methods and how a business depreciates its assets can affect how it makes money. This is discussed in more depth in Chapter 19, which covers business taxes.

Liabilities

On the balance sheet, the liabilities section includes the money the company owes to other businesses such as suppliers or lenders. Like the asset section, the liabilities section is divided into two parts: current liabilities and long-term liabilities.

Current liabilities are the debts the business must pay within the next year. Current liabilities include the accounts payable of the business as well as any loan payments due within the next year.

Accounts payable is the money the business owes to its suppliers. For instance, our retail store, Bonnie's Beachwear, purchased inventory to stock the store from wholesalers and manufacturers under terms that allowed the business 30 days to pay. During these 30 days, the business had an accounts payable on its balance sheet for these purchases.

Current liabilities can also include payroll expenses owed to employees, payments due for leased equipment, and any other bills the business hasn't yet paid.

The liabilities section of the balance sheet also includes the principal amount of any debt the business owes. The current assets section includes the debt that must be paid within one year. The long-term liabilities section includes the debt that must be paid in more than one year.

It's important to note that only the principal amount of the debt (i.e., the outstanding balance) gets included on the balance sheet. This is the amount the business borrowed. The interest on this debt is included on the profit and loss statement as an expense but is not included as a liability on the balance sheet.

The "Liabilities" chart below shows how the liabilities section of a balance sheet might look for a business with $30,000 of accounts payable and a $30,000 loan from a bank, where $5,000 of principal must be repaid in the current year and $25,000 must be repaid in subsequent years.

Typical Balance Sheet Liabilities

Liabilities	
Current Liabilities	
Accounts Payable	$30,000
Bank Loan Payable	$5,000
Total Current Liabilities	**$35,000**
Long-Term Liabilities	
Bank Loan Payable	$25,000
Total Long-Term Liabilities	**$25,000**
Total Liabilities	**$60,000**

Owners' Equity

The final section of the balance sheet is owners' equity (see page 101). Owners' equity is the value of the business after all its liabilities have been paid. If the assets of the business were to be sold, and the liabilities of the business paid, the owners' equity is the amount of money that would be left over for the owners.

OWNERS' EQUITY is the amount of money that would be LEFT OVER for the owners.

Like the other items on the balance sheet, owners' equity is calculated using the rules of accounting, including historical costs that may be more or less than current values. If the owners were to actually sell the business, they might receive more or less money for it than the owners' equity amount.

Owners' equity typically includes a section for the investment the owners and other equity investors have made into the business as well as a section for the business's retained earnings.

Owners' Investment

Any for-profit business starts out with the owners investing personal funds into the company to allow it to begin operations. This is the owners' equity investment.

As the business grows, others may invest in the business. This is also owners' equity investment—these investors own a piece of the business.

If the business grows even more, it may raise additional equity through the sale of stock. This, too, represents owners' equity investment as the stockholders own a piece of the business.

Owners' investment on the balance sheet includes the cumulative total of all the money that has been invested in the business by its owners. For a small business, this might solely be the money the owners invested. For a larger business, this could also include the money others have put into the business or the money the company has raised by selling stock.

Retained Earnings

The final item on the balance sheet is retained earnings. Retained earnings are the total of all the net profits of the business that haven't been paid as dividends to the owners.

Retained earnings are the cumulative profits of the business since its inception, which have been kept in the business (retained) and not paid to the owners.

Remember from Chapter 6 that profits are different than cash and are determined using the rules of accounting. As retained earnings are the cumulative profits of the business, retained earnings are also based on the rules of accounting. A business typically doesn't have its retained earnings available in cash, and as we showed in the examples in Chapter 6, a business can show a profit yet have no cash flow.

When a business earns a profit, that profit belongs to the owners of the business. The business can either pay all or a percentage of the profits to its owners in the form of dividends, or it can pay none of the profits to the owners. When the business is growing or cash flow is tight, it's quite common for a business not to pay dividends. More mature businesses, or those generating significant cash flow that isn't needed by the business, are more likely to pay dividends to the owners. Retained earnings include only the profits that haven't been paid to the owners as dividends.

Typical Balance Sheet
Owners' Equity

Owners' Equity	
Owners' Investment	$30,000
Retained Earnings	$10,000
Total Owners' Equity	**$40,000**

We've now built a complete balance sheet (below). In the next section, we'll look at the development of a balance sheet for our sample retail store, Bonnie's Beachwear.

Complete Balance Sheet

Assets

Current Assets

Cash	$10,000
Accounts Receivable	$30,000
Inventory	$10,000
Raw Materials	$5,000
Work in Process	$5,000
Total Current Assets	**$60,000**

Plant, Property and Equipment

Equipment	$50,000
Less: Accumulated Depreciation	($10,000)
Total Plant, Property and Equipment	**$40,000**
Total Assets	**$100,000**

Liabilities and Owners' Equity
Liabilities

Current Liabilities

Accounts Payable	$30,000
Bank Loan Payable	$5,000
Total Current Liabilities	**$35,000**

Long-Term Liabilities

Bank Loan Payable	$25,000
Total Long-Term Liabilities	**$25,000**
Total Liabilities	**$60,000**

Owners' Equity

Owners' Investment	$30,000
Retained Earnings	$10,000
Total Owners' Equity	**$40,000**
Total Liabilities and Owners' Equity	**$100,000**

Bonnie's Beachwear Balance Sheet

Now that Bonnie's Beachwear has had a chance to start up and operate for a few months, let's take a look at what a balance sheet might look like for our retail store.

Business Startup

In Chapter 2, we discussed some of the costs Bonnie would incur to start the store. Specifically, the business needed to spend $40,000 on furniture and fixtures to outfit the store and would also be spending $10,000 on computerized cash registers, an office computer, and inventory management software.

The purchase of each of these items creates an asset on the business's balance sheet. Both furniture and fixtures, and the computer equipment and software, become part of the business's plant, property and equipment assets.

To purchase these items, the business will need some startup capital, money that can be used to pay the business's startup expenses. Startup capital is typically obtained from a combination of loans and the owners' personal funds.

For this example, let's assume Bonnie invests $30,000 of her own funds in the business and borrows $30,000 from a bank for a total of $60,000 in startup capital. This will provide enough money to buy furniture and fixtures for the store, purchase the computers and software, and still leave $10,000 of cash available to the business.

Bonnie's $30,000 investment would be included in the owners' equity section of the balance sheet as owners' investment. The $30,000 loan from the bank would be included as a long-term liability in the liabilities section of the balance sheet.

From this $60,000, $50,000 is spent to pay for the store's furniture and fixtures and purchase the computer equipment and software. The remaining $10,000 is a cash asset on the balance sheet. As the "Startup Balance Sheet" shows (see page 104), the business has

$60,000 in assets (cash, furniture and fixtures, and equipment), and $60,000 in liabilities and owners' equity (a $30,000 loan and a $30,000 investment by the owner).

Bonnie's Beachwear Startup Balance Sheet

Assets

Current Assets

Cash	$10,000
Inventory	$0
Total Current Assets	**$10,000**

Plant, Property and Equipment

Equipment	$10,000
Furniture and Fixtures	$40,000
Total Plant, Property and Equipment	**$50,000**
Total Assets	**$60,000**

Liabilities and Owners' Equity
Liabilities

Current Liabilities

Accounts Payable	$0
Total Current Liabilities	**$0**

Long-Term Liabilities

Bank Loan Payable	$30,000
Total Long-Term Liabilities	**$30,000**
Total Liabilities	**$30,000**

Owners' Equity

Owners' Investment	$30,000
Retained Earnings	$0
Total Owners' Equity	**$30,000**
Total Liabilities and Owners' Equity	**$60,000**

Inventory Purchases

Additionally, before Bonnie's can open, it will need to purchase a supply of bathing suits and beachwear that can be sold to customers.

In discussing the cash flow statement for Bonnie's Beachwear in Chapter 3 and the profit and loss statement in Chapter 5, we noted that the wholesalers and manufacturers would be willing to ship merchandise to the store and allow the business 30 days to pay.

If Bonnie's were to purchase $18,000 worth of inventory before opening the store, the business could obtain the inventory now and pay for it in 30 days. During the 30 days, Bonnie's Beachwear could open for business, sell some of the inventory, and receive cash that could be used to pay for the inventory.

Assuming Bonnie's purchased $18,000 worth of inventory and planned to take 30 days to pay, the asset section of the balance sheet would show an inventory asset of $18,000, and the liability section would show an accounts payable liability of $18,000.

After the initial inventory has been purchased for Bonnie's Beachwear, the balance sheet would look like the sample on page 106 (see "Balance Sheet After Inventory Purchase"). Note that the assets of the business have increased by $18,000 as a result of the inventory purchase, and the liabilities have also increased by $18,000 since the store now owes additional money to its suppliers.

Of course, this also means that the business needs to open its doors and begin selling some products. It has only $10,000 in cash and owes $18,000 to its suppliers in 30 days.

Bonnie's Beachwear
Balance Sheet After Inventory Purchase

Assets
  Current Assets
    Cash $10,000
    Inventory $18,000
  Total Current Assets   **$28,000**

  Plant, Property and Equipment
    Equipment $10,000
    Furniture and Fixtures $40,000
  Total Plant, Property and Equipment   **$50,000**

Total Assets   **$78,000**

Liabilities and Owners' Equity
Liabilities
  Current Liabilities
    Accounts Payable $18,000
  Total Current Liabilities   **$18,000**

  Long-Term Liabilities
    Bank Loan Payable $30,000
  Total Long-Term Liabilities   **$30,000**

Total Liabilities   **$48,000**

Owners' Equity
  Owners' Investment $30,000
  Retained Earnings $0
Total Owners' Equity   **$30,000**

Total Liabilities and Owners' Equity   **$78,000**

Operating Activities

Now let's see what happens to the balance sheet of Bonnie's Beachwear after the business has been in operation for three months.

During these three months, several events have taken place:

- Bonnie's Beachwear has opened its doors and begun selling bathing suits and beachwear to customers.

- The business has purchased additional inventory to replace the merchandise it has sold and to keep the store stocked so customers have a selection of items from which to choose.

- The office equipment and furniture and fixtures have been depreciated.

- The business is experiencing a positive cash flow.

- The business has begun to make a profit.

Let's see how these events are reflected in the balance sheet, titled "After 3 Months of Operations," on page 108.

Bonnie's Beachwear Balance Sheet
After 3 Months of Operations

Assets

Current Assets	
Cash	$20,400
Inventory	$27,000
Total Current Assets	**$47,400**
Plant, Property and Equipment	
Equipment	$10,000
Less: Accumulated Depreciation	($600)
Furniture and Fixtures	$40,000
Less: Accumulated Depreciation	($2,400)
Total Plant, Property and Equipment	**$47,000**
Total Assets	**$94,400**
Liabilities and Owners' Equity	
Liabilities	
Current Liabilities	
Accounts Payable	$18,000
Total Current Liabilities	**$18,000**
Long-Term Liabilities	
Bank Loan Payable	$30,000
Total Long-Term Liabilities	**$30,000**
Total Liabilities	**$48,000**
Owners' Equity	
Owners' Investment	$30,000
Retained Earnings	$16,400
Total Owners' Equity	**$46,400**
Total Liabilities and Owners' Equity	**$94,400**

Inventory Purchases

To keep the store stocked with bathing suits, coverups and casual beachwear for customers, the business has purchased additional inventory to make sure it always has a good supply of merchandise.

On the balance sheet, we might see that Bonnie's Beachwear has more assets in inventory than it has liabilities in accounts payable. The inventory on the balance sheet would include merchandise just received from manufacturers and suppliers (and not yet paid for) as well as inventory received in prior months (which had been paid for).

In our example on page 108, Bonnie's balance sheet has $27,000 in inventory and $18,000 in accounts payable. The $27,000 reflects $18,000 in inventory received during the month (with payment due in 30 days) and $9,000 in inventory it already had on hand at the beginning of the month (which was paid for in a prior month).

Depreciation

The business will need to depreciate its office equipment and the furniture and fixtures in the store. The $10,000 equipment and software might be depreciated by $600, and the $40,000 in furniture and fixtures might be depreciated by $2,400 over these three months of operations.

On the balance sheet, the total value of plant, property and equipment assets has been reduced by $3,000, from $50,000 to $47,000, as a result of this depreciation.

Operations

If we assume that during these three months of operations, the business has become profitable, we will expect to see positive changes in both cash and retained earnings.

Cash has increased from $10,000 on the "Startup Balance Sheet" to $20,400 on the "After 3 Months of Operations Balance Sheet." This means that the business has generated $10,400 in cash from operations over this period.

Recall that retained earnings are the cumulative profits of the business since its inception. Retained earnings were zero at the startup of the business and have grown to $16,400 at the end of three months.

This means the cumulative net profits of the business over these three months were $16,400. In Chapter 5 we presented a sample profit and loss statement for Bonnie's Beachwear that showed the business made a net profit of $5,471 in one month, so earnings of $16,400 over three months is quite possible.

Overall, the assets of the business have grown from $74,000 at the start of operations to $94,400 at the end of three months, and most important, the value of the owners' investment in the business has grown from the initial $30,000 investment to $46,400.

In the next chapter, we'll look at the unique characteristics of manufacturers and service business balance sheets.

CHAPTER EIGHT

How the Balance Sheet Varies by Business Type

Before we conclude our discussion of balance sheets, we'd like to highlight one other important item: Some of the details of the assets and liabilities found on a balance sheet may vary for different types of businesses. In Chapter 7, we presented a balance sheet for a retail business. In this chapter, we'll look at how the balance sheets for a manufacturer and a service business might differ.

Manufacturing Business

Let's start by looking at a balance sheet for a manufacturing company. Again, we'll use our sample company, Boutique Handbags, as an example.

Background

As described in Chapter 2, Boutique Handbags is a manufacturer of designer women's handbags, which it sells to women's specialty stores and high-end department stores.

Boutique rents its manufacturing facility, but has purchased $20,000 worth of manufacturing equipment and $10,000 worth of computers and software. Boutique sells the handbags for $40 each. The handbags cost $20 each to manufacture, of which $12 is labor and $8 is materials cost.

The business experiences timing differences in the receipt and payment of cash flows. The business allows customers 60 days to pay for the handbags it has shipped, yet the business must pay for materials used in the manufacturing process in 30 days, and it must pay its workers weekly.

The ASSET SECTION of a manufacturing company's balance sheet is generally MORE EXTENSIVE.

Boutique tries to keep two weeks' supply of finished inventory on hand so it can quickly fill a customer's order. On a typical day, the business will also have a week's supply of raw materials and some handbags in the middle of the manufacturing process.

The cash to start the business and fund initial operations has come from a $40,000 investment by the owner and a $68,000 loan from a local bank.

Balance Sheet

The asset section of a manufacturing company's balance sheet is generally more extensive than the asset section of a retail business's or service business's balance sheet. (To see what Boutique Handbags' balance sheet looks like, check out the "Manufacturing Company Balance Sheet" on page 113.)

Boutique Handbags
Manufacturing Company Balance Sheet

Assets
    Current Assets

Cash	$16,000
Accounts Receivable	$80,000
Inventory	$10,000
Raw Materials	$2,000
Work in Process	$5,000
Total Current Assets	**$113,000**
Plant, Property and Equipment	
Equipment	$30,000
Less: Accumulated Depreciation	($3,000)
Total Plant, Property and Equipment	**$27,000**
Total Assets	**$140,000**
Liabilities and Owners' Equity	
Liabilities	
Current Liabilities	
Accounts Payable	$20,000
Total Current Liabilities	**$20,000**
Long-Term Liabilities	
Bank Loan Payable	$68,000
Total Long-Term Liabilities	**$68,000**
Total Liabilities	**$88,000**
Owners' Equity	
Owners' Investment	$40,000
Retained Earnings	$12,000
Total Owners' Equity	**$52,000**
Total Liabilities and Owners' Equity	**$140,000**

In our example for Boutique Handbags, two significant events are reflected in the asset section of the balance sheet. First, accounts receivable are a significant amount for this business. By allowing customers 60 days to pay, the business can ship two months' worth of products to customers before it receives payment.

Using this process, accounts receivable can grow very rapidly to a significant amount of money. In our example, if Boutique ships 1,000 handbags per month to customers at a price of $40 each, the business is shipping $40,000 worth of merchandise each month to customers. Over two months, accounts receivable would grow to $80,000.

Second, the asset section of the balance sheet includes the value of completed inventory that hasn't been shipped to customers, materials and labor costs of handbags that are in the middle of the manufacturing process, and the value of raw materials the business has on hand that haven't yet entered the manufacturing process. In our example, Boutique Handbags has $17,000 in inventory, raw materials, and work in process assets.

A manufacturing business can have a SIGNIFICANT amount of MONEY tied up in the manufacturing process.

Overall, as this example shows, a manufacturing business can have a significant amount of money tied up in the manufacturing process, inventory, and waiting for payment from customers. As a result, the liabilities and owners' equity section for a manufacturing company will need to include a large investment from the owners or a large loan from the bank so it has a source of funds for the assets.

In our example, Boutique's owner has invested $40,000 in the business, and the business has borrowed $68,000 from the bank. These funds allow the business to manufacture items ahead of sale and wait 60 days for payment from customers.

The difference in timing of the cash flows means that a manufacturing business will need proportionately more cash investment from the owners or the bank than will a retail or service business.

Similarities

The other entries on the balance sheet—cash; retained earnings; plant, property and equipment; and depreciation—are similar in content in a manufacturing business to those in a retail business.

Service Business

The balance sheet for a service business is often much simpler than the balance sheet for a manufacturing or retail business. After all, a service business typically doesn't have inventory and it wouldn't be engaged in the manufacture of products.

Background

As an example of a service business, let's use our doctor's office, Uptown Chiropractic. As described in Chapter 2, Uptown Chiropractic provides a full range of chiropractic services from its office in Alexandria, Virginia.

There are several things that are noteworthy about the business as they relate to the balance sheet. First, the business leases the treatment equipment used in patient treatments. Since the equipment is leased, it doesn't appear as an asset on the balance sheet and it isn't depreciated. Leased equipment is owned by the leasing company, appears on its balance sheet, and is depreciated on its balance sheet. The only plant, property and equipment assets of Uptown Chiropractic are the computer and software the business purchased.

Second, a significant portion of the business's revenue comes from insurance company reimbursement for services provided to patients. As was the case in our manufacturing company example, our service business must also wait to get paid and will also have significant accounts receivable on its balance sheet.

Uptown Chiropractic
Service Business Balance Sheet

Assets	
Current Assets	
Cash	$9,000
Inventory	$49,500
Total Current Assets	**$58,500**
Plant, Property and Equipment	
Equipment	$10,000
Less: Accumulated Depreciation	($500)
Total Plant, Property and Equipment	**$9,500**
Total Assets	**$68,000**
Liabilities and Owners' Equity	
Liabilities	
Current Liabilities	
Accounts Payable	$0
Total Current Liabilities	**$0**
Long-Term Liabilities	
Bank Loan Payable	$40,000
Total Long-Term Liabilities	**$40,000**
Total Liabilities	**$40,000**
Owners' Equity	
Owners' Investment	$20,000
Retained Earnings	$8,000
Total Owners' Equity	**$28,000**
Total Liabilities and Owners' Equity	**$68,000**

Balance Sheet

The balance sheet for Uptown Chiropractic is simpler than the balance sheet for Bonnie's Beachwear or Boutique Handbags (see "Service Business Balance Sheet" above). The business doesn't have inventory, and it doesn't have any accounts payable associated with paying for inventory. Because the business leases its treatment equipment and only owns its computers and software, its plant, property and equipment assets are small.

The most significant asset on the balance sheet is accounts receivable. Accounts receivable includes the payments the business is expecting from insurance companies in 120 days.

A key issue that Uptown Chiropractic faces is how to pay its expenses, most significantly the salaries of the owner and the two chiropractic assistants, while waiting to be reimbursed from the insurance companies.

For this reason, the liabilities and owners' equity section shows a $20,000 owners' investment in the business and a $40,000 bank loan. These provide the business the money it needs to operate while waiting for reimbursement from the insurance companies.

Service Business Cash Flow

The most common cash flow issue a service business faces is paying the expenses of the business while waiting for reimbursement from customers. In our example, Uptown Chiropractic must wait 120 days between the time it provides patient treatments and the time it receives payment from the insurance companies.

The BALANCE SHEET for a service business is often much SIMPLER.

Many service businesses face a similar issue. They provide a service to the customer on one day, but they don't receive payment until a later date. In between, they must pay staff salaries and the business's operating expenses.

For example, the authors of this book provide consulting services to individuals, companies and nonprofit organizations. While we, of course, would always like to be paid upfront, the client would like to pay at the end of the contract, and our contracts typically include a provision for final payment upon completion of the project. In between, we must pay the salaries of our staff and the operating expenses of our business.

While the basic structure of the balance sheet is the same for any type of business, as these examples have shown, the amount of assets and liabilities needed to operate a company can differ by type of business as can the individual asset and liability categories.

CHAPTER NINE

How Financial Statements Tie Together

The prior chapters introduced the cash flow statement, the profit and loss statement, and the balance sheet. In this chapter, we'll discuss how the numbers flow from one statement to another. That is, we'll explain how the financial statements tie together.

We'll start out by examining how the balance sheet and profit and loss statement, and the balance sheet and cash flow statement, tie together from the operating activities of the business. We'll follow that with a brief discussion of how financing activities and asset activities flow between the balance sheet and cash flow statement.

Operating Activities

Operating activities affect not only the cash flow and profits of the business; they also affect the entries on the balance sheet. Let's look at how operating activities flow through a business's financial statements. We'll start by discussing the flow between the balance sheet and the profit and loss statement, then wrap up the chapter by exploring the flow between the balance sheet and the cash flow statement.

Balance Sheet and Profit and Loss Statement

There are two numbers from the profit and loss statement that flow to the balance sheet: net profit and depreciation expense.

The net profit (or loss) from the bottom line of the profit and loss statement gets added to (or subtracted from, in the case of a loss) the retained earnings in the owners' equity section of the balance sheet. As we discussed in Chapter 7, retained earnings are the cumulative profits since the inception of the business that have been kept in the business (retained) and not paid to the owners of the business.

The NET PROFIT...gets added to... RETAINED EARNINGS.

At the end of each accounting period, the net profits from the profit and loss statement are added to the retained earnings in the owners' equity section of the balance sheet. If the business incurred a loss instead of a profit, the amount of the loss would be subtracted from the retained earnings on the balance sheet.

We discussed depreciation in both Chapters 5 and 7. In Chapter 5, we defined depreciation as a noncash operating expense on the profit and loss statement that allows a business to deduct the periodic wear and tear of its equipment and machinery. In Chapter 7, we showed how a business recorded accumulated depreciation as a deduction from its plant, property and equipment assets in the assets section of the balance sheet.

At the end of each accounting period, a business will recognize depreciation for that accounting period as an expense on its profit and loss statement, and that same depreciation amount will be added to the accumulated depreciation in the asset section of the balance sheet.

The graph below ("Tying Together the Balance Sheet and Profit and Loss Statement") shows the flow of net profit (or loss) from the profit and loss statement to the balance sheet and also shows the flow of the depreciation expense to the accumulated depreciation line in the asset section of the balance sheet.

Tying Together the Balance Sheet and Profit and Loss Statement

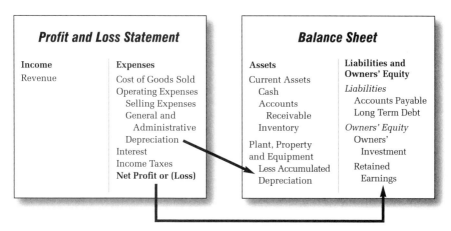

Now let's apply this knowledge to our sample retail business, Bonnie's Beachwear.

Bonnie's profit and loss statement on page 122 details operating activities for the month of December 2009. During the month, the business has a net profit of $5,471 and recognizes an $833 depreciation expense for the monthly depreciation of the store's furniture and fixtures and computer equipment.

Bonnie's Beachwear Profit and Loss Statement

	Dec. 2009
Sales Activities	
Revenue	$50,000
Cost of Goods Sold	$18,000
Gross Profit	**$32,000**
Operating Expenses	
Selling Expenses	$12,000
General and Administrative Expenses	$10,000
Depreciation	$833
Total Operating Expenses	$22,833
Operating Profit	**$9,167**
Interest	$750
Profit Before Taxes	**$8,417**
Income Taxes at 35%	$2,946
Net Profit	**$5,471**

Bonnie's balance sheets for November and December 2009 are on page 123. On these statements, note that the amount of accumulated depreciation on the balance sheet (which is a negative number since it's deducted from the value of the plant, property and equipment assets) has increased by $833 from November to December, reflecting the addition of the $833 depreciation expense from the December profit and loss statement. Retained earnings have also increased by $5,471 from November to December, reflecting the addition of the net profits from December.

Bonnie's Beachwear Balance Sheet	Ending Nov. 2009	Period Ending Dec. 2009	Period Change Nov. to Dec.
Assets			
Current Assets			
Cash	$36,096	$42,400	
Accounts Receivable	$0	$0	
Inventory	$27,000	$27,000	
Total Current Assets	**$63,096**	**$69,400**	
Plant, Property and Equipment			
Equipment	$50,000	$50,000	
Less: Accumulated Depreciation	($9,167)	($10,000)	**($833)**
Total Plant, Property and Equipment	**$40,833**	**$40,000**	
Total Assets	**$103,929**	**$109,400**	
Liabilities and Owners' Equity			
Liabilities			
Current Liabilities			
Accounts Payable	$18,000	$18,000	
Total Current Liabilities	**$18,000**	**$18,000**	
Long-Term Liabilities			
Loan from Bank	$30,000	$30,000	
Total Long-Term Liabilities	$30,000	$30,000	
Total Liabilities	**$48,000**	**$48,000**	
Owners' Equity			
Owners' Investment	$45,000	$45,000	
Retained Earnings	**$10,929**	**$16,400**	**$5,741**
Total Owners' Equity	**$55,929**	**$61,400**	
Total Liabilities and Owners' Equity	**$103,929**	**$109,400**	

Balance Sheet and Cash Flow Statement

Next, let's explore how the cash flow statement and the balance sheet tie together.

The first line on the cash flow statement shows a business's cash on hand at the beginning of the accounting period. The next lines on the cash flow statement show the cash inflows and cash outflows during the period, and the last line shows the cash on hand at the end of the accounting period.

The cash the business had on hand at the start of the accounting period should match the cash reported in the asset section of the balance sheet at the start of the period, and the cash on hand at the end of the period should match the cash reported on the balance sheet at the end of the period.

The graph below ("Tying Together the Balance Sheet and Cash Flow Statement") shows the flow of cash from the balance sheet's starting period to the beginning cash on hand on the cash flow statement, and from the ending cash on hand on the cash flow statement to the balance sheet's ending period.

Tying Together the Balance Sheet and Cash Flow Statement

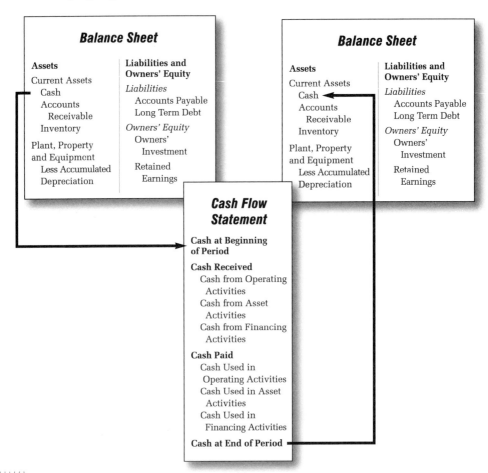

Let's again use the cash flow statement and balance sheet for Bonnie's Beachwear for an example (see the chart below). As of the end of November 2009, the business has $36,096 in cash.

Bonnie's Beachwear Balance Sheet	Period Ending Nov. 2009
Assets	
Current Assets	
Cash	$36,096
Accounts Receivable	$0
Inventory	$27,000
Total Current Assets	**$63,096**
Plant, Property and Equipment	
Equipment	$50,000
Less: Accumulated Depreciation	($9,167)
Total Plant, Property and Equipment	**$40,833**
Total Assets	**$103,929**
Liabilities and Owners' Equity	
Liabilities	
Current Liabilities	
Accounts Payable	$18,000
Total Current Liabilities	**$18,000**
Long-Term Liabilities	
Loan from Bank	$30,000
Total Long-Term Liabilities	**$30,000**
Total Liabilities	**$48,000**
Owners' Equity	
Owners' Investment	$45,000
Retained Earnings	$10,929
Total Owners' Equity	**$55,929**
Total Liabilities and Owners' Equity	**$103,929**

This $36,096 cash balance also appears as the cash on hand at the beginning period on the Bonnie's Beachwear December 2009 cash flow statement (see below).

Bonnie's Beachwear
Cash Flow Statement

	Dec. 2009
Cash at Beginning of Period	$36,096
Cash Received	
Cash from Operating Activities	
Cash Sales	$5,000
Collection of Check Sales	$5,000
Credit/Debit Card Sales	$40,000
Total Cash Received From Operating Activities	**$50,000**
Total Cash Received	**$50,000**
Cash Paid	
Cash Used in Operating Activities	
Inventory Costs	
Payments to Suppliers	$18,000
Selling	
Sales Staff	$10,000
Advertising	$2,000
General and Administrative	
Rent	$3,000
Utilities	$1,500
Owners' Salary	$4,500
Accounting, Payroll and Legal	$1,000
Income Taxes Paid	$2,946
Total Cash Used in Operating Activities	**$42,946**
Cash Used in Financing Activities	
Interest Paid	$750
Total Cash Used in Financing Activities	**$750**
Total Cash Paid	**$43,696**
Net Cash Flow	**$6,304**
Cash at End of Period	**$42,400**

During December, Bonnie's Beachwear receives $50,000 in cash from operating activities and pays out a total of $43,696 in cash, so during the month the business has a net cash flow of $6,304.

Bonnie's Beachwear ends December 2009 with $42,400 in cash. This $42,400 also appears on the cash balance in the asset section of Bonnie's Beachwear's December 2009 balance sheet (see below). The cash amount shown on the balance sheet is the same as the ending cash shown on the cash flow statement.

Bonnie's Beachwear **Balance Sheet**	Period Ending Nov. 2009	Period Ending Dec. 2009	Period Change Nov. to Dec.
Assets			
Current Assets			
Cash	**$36,096**	**$42,400**	**$6,304**
Accounts Receivable	$0	$0	
Inventory	$27,000	$27,000	
Total Current Assets	**$63,096**	**$69,400**	
Plant, Property and Equipment			
Equipment	$50,000	$50,000	
Less: Accumulated Depreciation	**($9,167)**	**($10,000)**	
Total Plant, Property and Equipment	**$40,833**	**$40,000**	
Total Assets	**$103,929**	**$109,400**	
Liabilities and Owners' Equity			
Liabilities			
Current Liabilities			
Accounts Payable	$18,000	$18,000	
Total Current Liabilities	**$18,000**	**$18,000**	
Long-Term Liabilities			
Loan from Bank	$30,000	$30,000	
Total Long-Term Liabilities	$30,000	$30,000	
Total Liabilities	**$48,000**	**$48,000**	
Owners' Equity			
Owners' Investment	$45,000	$45,000	
Retained Earnings	$10,929	$16,400	
Total Owners' Equity	**$55,929**	**$61,400**	
Total Liabilities and Owners' Equity	**$103,929**	**$109,400**	

Financing Activities

The startup cash flow of a business also affects the cash flow statement and the balance sheet. Let's start by looking at the business's financing activities.

The startup of any business requires some type of investment by the owner. In our example of Bonnie's Beachwear in Chapter 7, we assumed that Bonnie invested $30,000 of her own money into the business and also obtained a $30,000 loan from the bank.

The owners' investment and the money obtained from the bank are recognized as cash received from financing activities on the cash flow statement.

After the owner invests her money and the loan from the bank is received, the business has $60,000 in cash that appears as an asset on the balance sheet, $30,000 in liabilities (its debt to the bank), and $30,000 in owners' equity (Bonnie's investment in the business).

The startup investments in the business are included as financing activities on the cash flow statement and are included as cash in the asset section of the balance sheet as well as obligations of the business in the liabilities and owners' equity sections.

The graph on page 129 ("How Financing Activity Flows") shows the flow of the initial owners' investment and bank financing as it flows through the cash flow statement to the balance sheet.

How Financing Activity Flows

Cash Flow Statement

Cash at Beginning of Period

Cash Received
Cash from Operating Activities
Cash from Asset Activities
Cash from Financing Activities

Cash Paid
Cash Used in Operating Activities
Cash Used in Asset Activities
Cash Used in Financing Activities

Cash at End of Period

Owners' Investment

Loan from Bank

Balance Sheet

Assets	Liabilities and Owners' Equity
Current Assets	*Liabilities*
Cash	Accounts Payable
Accounts Receivable	Long-Term Debt
Inventory	*Owners' Equity*
Plant, Property and Equipment	Owners' Investment
Less Accumulated Depreciation	Retained Earnings

Asset Activities

Finally, let's look at the effect asset activities have on the balance sheet and cash flow statement. In our example of the startup of Bonnie's Beachwear (detailed in Chapter 7), the business used $50,000 of its startup money to outfit its store and purchase computer equipment.

The business began with $60,000 in cash, spent $50,000 to outfit the store and purchase the equipment, and ended with $10,000 in cash and $50,000 invested in plant, property, and equipment.

The graph on page 130 ("How Asset Activity Flows") shows these events graphically. Fifty thousand dollars flows from the cash assets on the balance sheet to the cash used in the asset activities section of the cash flow statement. The cash is spent to pay for the costs of outfitting the store and the computer equipment. These activities then flow back to the balance sheet as plant, property and equipment assets.

How Asset Activity Flows

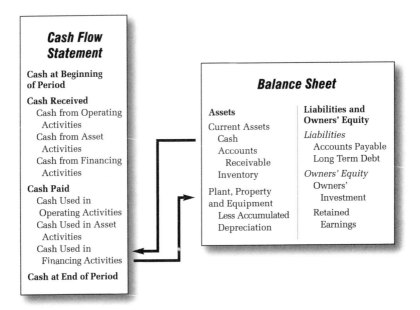

In this example, we've shown how money flows from cash, through the asset activities section of the cash flow statement, and into new plant, property and equipment assets on the balance sheet for the startup of a business. These same events occur when the business purchases additional assets that will be used in the operation of the business. The money will flow from cash, through asset activities, and into plant, property and equipment.

As we demonstrated in this chapter, all the primary financial statements of a business tie together, and as shown in the following examples, certain values flow from one financial statement to another:

- The profit or loss of a business gets added to the retained earnings of the business on the balance sheet.

- The depreciation expense on the profit and loss statement affects the accumulated depreciation on the balance sheet.

- The cash a business receives from financing activities flows to the cash balance of the business on the balance sheet and then flows from the cash balance when it's used for asset purchases.

- The cash balance on the balance sheet should match the ending cash position on the cash flow statement.

Now that we've provided an overview of the basic financial statements and demonstrated how those statements might look for our sample companies, we will next show how the information on the financial statements can be used to help you understand your business and create and manage a profitable company.

Part Three

Tools to Help You Make Money

The key to creating and managing a profitable business is understanding and using the information contained in the financial statements of the business.

In Part 3, we introduce a series of tools—ratios and other calculations that can be used to help you understand the financial operations of your business—as well as discuss how you can use this knowledge of your business's finances to evaluate the effectiveness of your operating strategies and compare your business to your competitors and to the industry.

CHAPTER TEN

Evaluating Profitability

 Now that you have a handle on the content of financial statements, let's turn to profitability. Understanding how to measure a company's profitability is very important to the success of your company. In this chapter, we'll present a series of tools—profitability ratios—that business owners and managers can use to measure a company's profitability, then we'll show you how to use the results from these calculations to identify financial trends in your company. We'll also show you how to perform an industry analysis, comparing the operations strategies of your business to your industry and to your competitors.

Profitability Ratios

There are five key profitability ratios:

- Gross margin
- Operating margin
- Net margin
- Return on assets
- Return on equity

The first three of these ratios measure the business's profitability resulting from its operating activities, while the last two measure the profitability from the perspective of its owners and investors. Let's address them one by one.

Gross Margin

Gross margin measures the relationship between revenue and gross profit. Gross margin tells you how much profit the business makes from each sale.

The formula for gross margin is gross profit divided by revenue.

$$\textbf{\textit{Gross Margin}} = \frac{\textbf{\textit{Gross Profit}}}{\textbf{\textit{Revenue}}}$$

Gross margin is typically expressed as a percentage. This means that rather than expressing the result of this calculation as a decimal number (e.g., 0.64), the result is typically expressed as a percentage (e.g., 64 percent). This can be done very simply by formatting the cell as a percentage in Excel, or by multiplying the result by 100 if you're doing the calculation using a calculator or by hand.

Gross margin is calculated using information from the sales activities section of the profit and loss statement. As you'll recall from Chapter 5, gross profit is calculated by deducting cost of goods sold or cost of services from revenue. Gross profit is the total amount of money the business made selling goods or services after paying for those goods or services. To determine how profitable the business is from each sale, gross profit is compared to sales revenue, and the resulting value is gross margin.

Gross margin tells you what percentage of each sales dollar is retained by the business. The sales dollars retained by the business are available to pay operating expenses and for payment to the owners as profit.

BY ANY OTHER NAME

Like many of the terms used in finance, gross margin is known by several different names. Gross margin is also known as *gross profit margin*, *gross profit margin percentage*, *gross margin percentage*, and *gross markup*.

Gross Margin at Bonnie's Beachwear

Let's look at the gross margin for Bonnie's Beachwear. In Chapter 5, we presented some examples of a profit and loss statement for Bonnie's Beachwear. In our examples, the business purchased bathing suits and beachwear at an average cost of $18 and sold these items for an average price of $50. If the business sold 1,000 items during the month, revenue would be $50,000, cost of goods sold would be $18,000, and gross profit would be $32,000.

Using this information, we can calculate a gross margin of 64 percent for Bonnie's Beachwear. This is calculated by dividing the gross profit of $32,000 by the revenue of $50,000. The result of this calculation is 0.64, which when expressed as a percentage is 64 percent ($32,000/$50,000 = 0.64 = 64%). (See below for the gross margin calculation for Bonnie's Beachwear).

Bonnie's Beachwear Gross Margin Calculation

Sales Activities		
Revenue	$50,000	
Cost of Goods Sold	$18,000	
Gross Profit	**$32,000**	**64%**

A 64-percent gross margin means that for every dollar of sales revenue earned by Bonnie's Beachwear, the business retains 64 cents.

Understanding Gross Margin

If you analyze the profit and loss statement of your own business and find that your gross margin is 64 percent, how do you know if this gross margin is good or bad? How do you know how you compare to your competitors? Are you more profitable or less profitable than the competition?

In this section, we'll show you how you can find out. We'll discuss the gross margins earned by different types of businesses.

Gross margin tells you how much PROFIT the BUSINESS makes from each sale.

Gross margins vary tremendously depending on the type of business and the kinds of products sold. You may have heard the terms "high-margin business" and "low-margin business." These terms refer to the gross margins earned by different types of businesses.

In Chapter 1, we discussed the four types of strategies a business can use to compete in the marketplace (innovation and design, operations, sales and marketing, and customer service) and how a business needs to be either customer-centric or operational-centric.

Pursuing a customer-centric approach allows a business to be a high-margin business. Customer-centric businesses use innovation and design, sales and marketing, and customer service as their business strategies. Businesses that use these strategies are often able to position their product as a premium product in the minds of customers, which allows for premium pricing. This premium pricing translates to a higher gross margin.

Operational-centric businesses are most often low-margin businesses because they focus on producing products as efficiently as possible. Operational-centric businesses tend to be found in more mature, established industries where price is a customer's primary consideration. As a result, operational-centric businesses have lower gross margins.

According to data provided by the U.S. Census Bureau, the average gross margin for retailers in the United States is 27.7 percent. But this gross margin varies tremendously for different types of retailers. Some retailers earn gross margins as high as 75 percent, while others earn gross margins as low as 15 percent.

The highest gross margins are earned by clothing stores and home furnishing retailers. In these businesses, gross margins of 45 to 50 percent are typical. High-end clothing stores often earn gross margins between 65 and 75 percent. The customer-centric focus of these businesses allows the retailer to charge a higher price for its products. Other specialty stores, such as sporting goods, hobby, book, and music stores also earn above-average gross margins, near 40 percent.

At the low end are the gross margins earned by gasoline stations and motor vehicle and auto-parts dealers. Here, gross margins of between 15 and 20 percent are more typical. These are followed by food and beverage stores, where the gross margins are between 27 and 29 percent.

Pursuing a CUSTOMER-CENTRIC approach allows a business to be a HIGH-MARGIN business.

There's also significant variance in gross margin among department stores. The lowest gross margins (20 percent) are earned by warehouse clubs and superstores, where price is the customer's primary consideration, and the highest gross margins (35 to 37 percent) are earned by full-service department stores, where the focus of the business may be more customer-centric. Finally, non-store retailers such as internet retailers and mail order companies earn gross margins between 38 and 39 percent.

For a summary of the gross margins earned by various categories of retailers, see "Gross Margins Earned by Retailers" on page 140. Our website, www.FinanceWithoutFear.com, contains additional data on the gross margins earned by various types of businesses.

Gross Margins Earned by Retailers	Gross Margin
Type of Business	
Retail Sales (All Types)	27.7%
Motor vehicle and parts dealers	18.3%
Furniture and home furnishings stores	46.6%
Electronics and appliance stores	28.0%
Building materials and garden equipment and supplies dealers	32.7%
Food and beverage stores	29.0%
Health and personal-care stores	29.7%
Gas stations	14.9%
Clothing and clothing accessory stores	45.7%
Sporting goods, hobby, book and music stores	40.5%
General merchandise stores	25.6%
Department stores (except discount dept. stores)	37.4%
Warehouse clubs and superstores	20.0%
Misc. store retailers	44.0%
E-commerce and mail order houses	38.5%

Source: U.S. Census Bureau

The gross margin for manufacturers also varies widely. Manufacturers that produce unique and innovative products earn the highest gross margins. Pharmaceutical companies, whose products are often protected with patents, can earn gross margins greater than 80 percent. It's not atypical for a manufacturer of scientific or medical equipment to earn gross margins greater than 70 percent. Consumer-product manufacturers that have used a sales and marketing strategy and developed strong name recognition in the market can earn gross margins of 50 percent or more.

Gross margins of 30 to 40 percent are typical for other types of manufacturers. This is particularly true for competitive industries where the focus is operational-centric. For instance, the gross margin for clothing manufacturers is approximately 38 percent, the gross margin for food manufacturers is approximately 37 percent, and the gross margin for equipment manufacturers is approximately 32 percent.

Wholesalers fill a vital role in the marketplace, distributing products produced by manufacturers to retailers. Wholesalers are the classic "middlemen." As a group, wholesalers earn the lowest gross margins. Wholesale gross margins range from lows of 6 percent for farm and petroleum products to highs of approximately 27 or 28 percent for machinery, equipment and home furnishings.

Overall, wholesalers of durable goods (machinery, equipment, computers, building materials and electrical products) earn gross margins of 23 percent, and wholesalers of nondurable goods (food, beverages, fuels, clothing, drugs and paper products) earn gross margins of 14 percent.

OPERATIONAL-CENTRIC businesses are most often LOW-MARGIN businesses.

Service businesses earn the highest gross margins, ranging from a low of 50 percent to a high of 80 percent or more. Service businesses don't have costs of goods sold, but they do have significant labor costs associated with providing their services. As we discussed in Chapter 5, the decision as to whether to allocate labor costs as a cost of services or as an operating expense can have a significant effect on a service business's gross margin. This makes gross margins somewhat difficult to compare across different service businesses. Fortunately, regardless of how labor costs are allocated in a service business, the operating margins of the businesses will be comparable.

So is 64 percent a good or bad gross margin for Bonnie's Beachwear? A 64-percent gross margin is high for a clothing retailer in general, but it's below the gross margin earned by some high-end clothing stores. Given that Bonnie's Beachwear is focused on a higher-end clientele, a 64-percent gross margin can be considered acceptable.

Operating Margin

Operating margin measures the relationship between revenue and a business's operating profit. This ratio tells you how profitable the business is from operations. Like gross margin, it too is typically expressed as a percentage.

Operating profit and revenue data used to calculate operating margin can be found on the profit and loss statement. The formula for operating margin is operating profit divided by revenue.

$$\text{Operating Margin} = \frac{\text{Operating Profit}}{\text{Revenue}}$$

In many ways, operating margin is a more meaningful measure of profitability because it measures profitability after all the operating expenses of the business have been included.

BY ANY OTHER NAME

Operating profit is also known as *earnings before interest and taxes*, or *EBIT*.

Operating margin also allows the comparison of businesses that are using different operating strategies. Businesses that use customer-centric strategies incur higher operating costs than do operational-centric businesses. If a business uses an innovation and design strategy, it will incur higher operating costs to pay its staff or to fund its research and development efforts. If a business uses a sales and marketing strategy, it will incur higher costs to advertise and market its products, and businesses that use a customer service strategy will, in turn, have higher customer service costs. An operating margin measures profitability using the profit of the business after these higher operating costs have been deducted.

Interest, taxes, and extraordinary income and expense items are excluded when calculating operating margin since these values can vary depending on the capital structure and company location, and aren't directly related to business operations.

BY ANY OTHER NAME

Operating margin is also known as *operating margin percentage*, *operating profit margin*, and *operating profit margin percentage*.

Operating Margin at Bonnie's Beachwear

As we discussed in Chapter 5, the monthly operating expenses for Bonnie's Beachwear are $22,833. After subtracting these operating expenses from profit, the business has an operating profit of $9,167.

An operating margin of 18 percent for Bonnie's Beachwear is calculated by dividing the $9,167 operating profit by the $50,000 monthly revenue ($9,167/$50,000 = 18%).

Bonnie's Beachwear Operating Margin Calculation

Sales Activities		
Revenue	$50,000	
Cost of Goods Sold	$18,000	
Gross Profit	**$32,000**	**64%**
Operating Expenses		
Selling Expenses		
Advertising	$2,000	
Sales Staff Salary	$10,000	
General and Administrative		
Rent	$3,000	
Utilities	$1,500	
Owners' Salary	$4,500	
Accounting, Payroll and Legal	$1,000	
Depreciation	$833	
Operating Profit	**$9,167**	**18%**

An 18-percent operating margin means that for every dollar of sales, after paying for the cost of the goods sold and operating expenses, the business retains 18 cents. (See above for the operating margin calculation for Bonnie's Beachwear.)

Understanding Operating Margin

We have the same questions about the operating margin for Bonnie's Beachwear as we did about the gross margin. Is an 18 percent operating margin good or bad? Is it better or worse than the competition?

Operating margins also vary by industry and can vary depending on the effectiveness of the strategy used by the business. When a business uses a customer-centric strategy, it must convince its customers to pay a premium price for its products. When the customer pays a premium price, the business may also generate an operating margin that is higher than the competition.

If the business isn't able to obtain a premium price from the customer, or has significantly increased its operating expenses in order to implement its strategy, the business may not achieve an operating margin that's higher than the competition. Likewise, a business using an operational-centric strategy will only achieve higher margins than its competitors when its operating expenses are lower than its competitors' operating expenses.

Operating margin...tells you how PROFITABLE the business is from operations.

A successful business has both a strong gross margin and a strong operating margin. Let's look at some industry data to get a sense of operating margins for different types of businesses.

We see a similar pattern with operating margins as we did with gross margins. Operating margins tend to be highest for businesses that use innovation and design, sales and marketing, and customer service strategies.

Operating margins for pharmaceutical companies, makers of medical and scientific equipment, and manufacturers of other unique and innovative products can be 20 to 25 percent, or higher for efficient manufacturers, and can be as low as 10 percent for manufacturers with higher operating expenses.

For manufacturers of consumer products and household goods, operating margins range from 10 to 25 percent. The highest operating margins are achieved by businesses that focus on a sales and marketing strategy and have efficient operations. Lower margins are achieved by businesses that operate less efficiently or that don't have established brand names.

Operating margins for service businesses are heavily dependent on the costs of providing those services. The norm is from 10 to 25 percent, with the highest operating margins being earned by businesses that offer unique or innovative services, have barriers to entry, or require licensing or other professional designations.

For retailers, operating margins typically range from 10 to 25 percent, with the highest operating margins achieved by retailers that focus on the high end of the market and operate efficiently, and the lowest operating margins obtained by operational-centric retailers who compete solely on price. Standard operating margins for many retailers are between 14 and 18 percent.

**A SUCCESSFUL business has both
a strong GROSS MARGIN and
a strong OPERATING MARGIN.**

The lowest operating margins tend to be earned by automobile retailers and food and beverage stores. The operating margins for these businesses are between 2 and 5 percent, with the highest margins earned by retailers that have strong brand recognition or that operate efficiently.

In our example, Bonnie's Beachwear earned an operating margin of 18 percent. Is that good or bad? As we've shown, high-end retailers can earn operating margins near 25 percent, and the operating margins for many retailers can hover near 18 percent. So an operating margin of 18 percent for a startup retailer, focused on a higher-end clientele, can be considered acceptable.

Net Margin

Net margin measures the relationship between a business's revenue and its net profits. This ratio tells you how profitable the business is after interest, taxes, and all extraordinary expenses have been paid. The formula for net margin is net profit divided by revenue.

$$\textit{Net Margin} = \frac{\textit{Net Profit}}{\textit{Revenue}}$$

Net margin is typically expressed as a percentage, and like gross margin and operating margin, the data used to calculate net margin can be found on the profit and loss statement.

Net margin tells you how profitable the company's bottom line is and allows for comparison to businesses in other industries.

BY ANY OTHER NAME

Net margin is also known as *net margin percentage, net profit margin,* and *net profit margin percentage.*

Net Margin at Bonnie's Beachwear

As we discussed in Chapter 5, we've assumed that Bonnie's Beachwear has an interest expense of $750 per month. Subtracting this interest expense from operating profit results in a profit before taxes of $8,417. Assuming a 35 percent tax rate, the business will owe $2,946 in taxes, and the net profit is $5,471.

Using this information, we can calculate a net margin of 11 percent ($5,471/$50,000 = 11%). This means for every dollar of sales, Bonnie's Beachwear makes a net profit of 11 cents. (See the net profit and net margin calculations in the chart on page 148.)

Bonnie's Beachwear Net Margin Calculation

Sales Activities		
Revenue	$50,000	
Cost of Goods Sold	$18,000	
Gross Profit	**$32,000**	**64%**
Operating Expenses		
Selling Expenses		
Advertising	$2,000	
Sales Staff Salary	$10,000	
General and Administrative		
Rent	$3,000	
Utilities	$1,500	
Owners' Salary	$4,500	
Accounting, Payroll and Legal	$1,000	
Depreciation	$833	
Operating Profit	**$9,167**	**18%**
Interest	$750	
Profit Before Taxes	**$8,417**	
Income Taxes @ 35%	$2,946	
Net Profit	**$5,471**	**11%**

Understanding Net Margin

The primary difference between net margin and operating margin is that net margin is calculated on the net profits of the business after interest, taxes, and any extraordinary items have been deducted. Since most small businesses pay taxes at similar rates, the key difference between net margin and operating margin results from interest.

Borrowing money and paying interest on this borrowed money is a decision that must be made by each individual business owner. Some businesses will borrow to finance their operations and growth, while others will pursue a more conservative, slower growth approach, and use the cash flow generated from operations of the business. Some businesses will borrow money to purchase equipment and pay interest on these borrowings, while others will lease the same equipment and not make interest payments.

NET MARGIN...allows for comparison to businesses in OTHER INDUSTRIES.

As a result, the interest expenses of businesses in the same industry can vary widely, based on each company's borrowing and operations strategies. Net margin allows the comparison of businesses after the effects of borrowing and operations decisions. In many instances, businesses with the highest operating margins will also have the highest net margins. Pharmaceutical companies, makers of medical and scientific equipment, and manufacturers of other unique and innovative products can earn net margins between 15 and 20 percent. Many manufacturers, however, earn net margins between 7 and 12 percent.

High-end retailers can also earn net margins between 15 and 20 percent. Most retailers, however, don't earn net margins this high. Overall, clothing stores earn net margins of 8 percent; home and electronics stores, near 4.5 percent; and department stores, between 4.5 and 5 percent.

Car dealers and gas stations earn the lowest retail net margins, where rates of 1.5 to 1.7 percent are typical. The net margins for food and beverage retailers aren't much better. The average net margin for food and beverage stores is 3 percent. Even the most successful food and beverage retailers earn net margins below 5 percent, and some are below 1 percent.

The net margins for service businesses range from 5 to 15 percent, with the highest operating margins earned by companies that offer unique or innovative services, have barriers to entry, or require licensing or other professional designations. Net margins in the entertainment business are 14 to 15 percent, while lawyers earn 12 percent and accountants, 9 percent. Banks, health-care providers, and advertising agencies made lower net margins, between 7 and 8 percent.

In our example, Bonnie's Beachwear earned a net margin of 11 percent. Once again, this net margin is probably very typical for a retailer focused on a high-end clientele. This net margin is below that earned by the established high-end retailers, yet is above the net margin for a typical clothing store. An 11-percent net margin seems to be acceptable for this business.

Analyzing Your Margins

Gross margin, operating margin and net margin can provide valuable information that can help your business make money. By calculating margins, you're able to see the percentage of profits your business makes from each sale, after paying operating expenses, and after all other expenses and taxes are paid. The calculation and review of your margins allows you to compare your company to your industry and your competitors, and to analyze the reasons for the changes in the profitability of your business.

Industry Analysis

In general, businesses that sell similar products and services earn margins that are typical for that industry. An analysis of the margins for a business or industry can tell you the strategies used and how businesses in that industry make money. For instance:

- Food and beverage retailers have low margins. They make a small amount of money on each sale. In order to make money, food and beverage retailers must have a significant sales volume and be operationally efficient.

- The margins for clothing retailers are among the highest of all retailers. Clothing retailers make more money on each sale than do food and beverage retailers, but they also sell fewer items. In order to make money, a clothing retailer must use a customer-centric strategy and sufficiently differentiate its products so customers are willing to pay premium prices.

- Manufacturing businesses that rely on innovation and design to differentiate their products also earn high margins. Their products must be differentiated such that customers are willing to pay a premium price for those products.

- Manufacturing businesses that rely on operational-centric strategies earn lower margins and make money through operational efficiency rather than through premium prices.

In order to structure your company to make money, you need to understand the margins of other businesses in your industry, and you need to understand how your business is both the same and different.

For your business to earn higher margins than are typical for the industry, you should be able to define how your business is different, and be able to define the strategies you'll use to earn these higher margins.

If your business operates using the same strategies as your competitors, it will be very difficult to earn higher margins than your competitors. To earn higher margins, a business needs to have a competitive advantage. This is key to making money.

Trend Analysis

It's also important to understand how your margins are changing over time and what these changes mean to your business's profitability. In order to spot trends affecting their businesses early, many companies conduct monthly, weekly, or even daily analysis of their margins.

An increase in your gross margin indicates the business is now earning more gross profit on each sale. This could be the result of an increase in your prices, a change in your product mix to higher gross margin products, or a decrease in your cost of goods sold or cost of services.

A decrease in your gross margin indicates that the business is now earning less gross profit on each sale. This could be the result of a decrease in your prices, a change in your product mix toward lower gross margin products, or an increase in your costs of goods sold or cost of services that you didn't pass through to the customer in the form of a price increase.

Gross Margin Trends

Trend	Possible Cause
Increase in Gross Margin	Price Increase Change in product mix to higher gross margin products Decrease in cost of goods sold or cost of services
Decrease in Gross Margin	Price decrease Change in product mix to lower gross margin products Increase in cost of goods sold or cost of services

---

Decreases in gross margin indicate that a business should review its pricing and cost of goods sold or cost of services. Oftentimes, a change in gross margin will also result in a change to operating margin and net margin. If a business is now earning more on each sale, operating profit and net profit should also be higher. If a business earns less on each sale, operating profit and net profit would be expected to be lower.

A change in operating margin without a change in gross margin indicates a change in the business's operating expenses. If the operating margin decreases, this would indicate an increase in operating expenses. If the operating margin increases, this would indicate a decrease in operating expenses.

Operating Margin Trends

Trend	Possible Cause
Increase in Operating Margin	Increase in Gross Margin Decrease in Operating Expenses
Decrease in Operating Margin	Decrease in Gross Margin Increase in Operating Expenses

If operating margin decreases, and operating expenses have increased, the reasons for the rise in operating expenses should be reviewed because if the trend continues, the business will make less money.

Finally, changes in net margin will generally correspond to changes in operating margin. However, net margin can be affected by changes in interest costs that might result from the financing activities of the business, changes in tax rates, or from one-time extraordinary items.

Return on Assets

The profitability of a business can also be measured by the returns it generates. Return on assets is one way to measure the returns from the operations of the business. This ratio measures the relationship between the net profit of the business and the assets it uses to produce the net profit. Return on assets tells you how effective you were in using those assets to generate a profit for the business.

The formula for return on assets is net profit divided by total assets.

$$\text{Return on Assets} = \frac{\text{Net Profit}}{\text{Total Assets}}$$

Return on assets tells you what percentage of every dollar invested in assets is returned as profit. This ratio is typically expressed as an annual return. For example, if the total assets of a business are $125,000, and annual net profit is $10,000, the return on assets is 8.0% ($10,000/$125,000 = 8.0%).

BY ANY OTHER NAME

Return on assets is also commonly referred to as *ROA*.

Understanding Return on Assets

Return on assets measures how effectively the business is using its assets. This ratio is particularly important for businesses that have a significant investment in plant, property and equipment, or have significant accounts receivable. It costs money to acquire assets, so a business will want to use its assets efficiently to generate the highest return possible from them.

Generating the highest return often means using the assets as frequently as possible. For example, a manufacturing business will often run two shifts in a single factory rather than build a second factory. A retail store will open early in the day and close late at night to allow as many customers as possible to visit the store.

This maximizes asset use and minimizes the costs of acquiring new assets. A business that adds a second shift or stays open later can increase net profit without adding assets. This increased net profit will greatly increase its return on assets.

Return on assets tends to be lowest in industries where a significant investment in plant, property and equipment is needed to compete, and it tends to be highest in industries where there's not a significant investment in plant, property and equipment.

For service businesses, return on assets tends to be high, as service businesses very often have a minimal investment in plant, property and equipment. Conversely, return on assets might be low for a manufacturing business that has invested heavily in manufacturing equipment or in a factory building.

How a business acquires the equipment used in its production processes can also have an effect on return on assets. A business that leases its equipment will have a smaller total asset size than a company that has purchased its equipment. Hence, the business that leases its equipment will have a larger return on assets than the business that purchases its equipment.

Likewise, return on assets can vary for retail businesses, depending on the strategies they use to acquire stores. Return on assets will be lower for a retail business that has purchased its store building than for one that rents its store.

Return on Equity

Return on equity is another profitability ratio that shows the returns from the operations of the business. This ratio measures the relationship between the net profit of a business and the owners' equity in the business. Return on equity tells the owner how effective the business was in generating a return on his/her investment.

The formula for return on equity is net profit divided by owners' equity.

$$\textbf{\textit{Return on Equity}} = \frac{\textbf{\textit{Net Profit}}}{\textbf{\textit{Owners' Equity}}}$$

Return on equity tells you what percentage of profit you make for every dollar of equity invested in the business. The owners can use return on equity to compare their investment in this business with other investments.

Like return on assets, return on equity is normally expressed as a percentage and is typically expressed as an annual return, calculated using annual net profit. For example, if the owners' equity in a business is $100,000 and the net profit is $10,000, the return on assets is 10.0% ($10,000/$100,000 = 10.0%).

BY ANY OTHER NAME

Return on equity is also known as *ROE*.

Understanding Return on Equity

Return on equity measures the return the business provides to its owners. A business owner can use return on equity to compare investment alternatives, such as the return from investing in the business vs. the return from investing in a different business, or vs. the return from leaving the money in the bank or the stock market.

Return on equity generated by a business is highly dependent on the relative percentages of debt and owners' equity used to finance the business. Conservative businesses tend to use more owners' equity and less debt, while leveraged (or aggressive) businesses tend to use more debt and less equity to finance the business. A leveraged business can earn a higher return on equity, but it's also taking a greater risk since the business must generate sufficient operating profits to repay the debt.

If a given business earned a $10,000 profit, and it was financed with $100,000 in owners' equity, the return on equity would be 10 percent. If the same business were financed with $50,000 of owners' equity and $50,000 in debt, the return on equity would be 20 percent. If the business was highly leveraged, with $20,000 of owners' equity and $80,000 in debt, the return on equity would be 50 percent.

While return on equity allows for comparison to other businesses or to other investments, the debt and owners' equity combination used by the business can affect the results and needs to be considered when using this ratio as a comparative tool.

Return on equity is one of the criteria an investor uses when deciding whether or not to invest in a business. This will be discussed further in Chapter 21.

As you can see, profitability ratios provide valuable information that allow you to not only calculate the profitability of your company but to also spot trends affecting your business and to evaluate the effectiveness of your strategies as well as the returns generated by your business.

SOURCES OF INDUSTRY DATA

There are several sources of industry average margin and return data. The *U.S. Census Bureau* provides several online sources:

- *Gross margin and operating expense data for the retail industry:* www.census.gov/retail/
- *Gross margin data for U.S. wholesalers:* www.census.gov/wholesale/index.html
- *Operating activity and expense data for retail, manufacturing, service, and wholesale business from the U.S. Economic Census:* www.census.gov/econ/index.html

Additionally, the *Finance Without Fear* website (www.FinanceWithoutFear.com) includes a series of downloadable tables with gross margin, operating margin and net margin data.

It's also possible to calculate gross, operating, and net margins, and return on asset and equity for publicly traded companies using publicly available financial statement data.

Online sources of data for public companies include the Fortune 500 list and the Securities and Exchange Commission database.

(continued on next page)

- *Fortune 500:* The list of the 500 largest companies in the United States is an excellent source of industry data, which can be used to calculate margins and returns. Summary financial information for the companies included in the Fortune 500 can be found at http://money.cnn.com/magazines/fortune/fortune500/2010/full_list/. Margins and returns for select companies can be calculated using the financial statement data for these companies.

- *Public Information:* All public companies are required to file copies of their financial statements with the Securities and Exchange Commission (the "SEC"), and these filings become public record. The revenue, gross profit, operating profit, and net profit data needed to calculate gross margin, operating margin, and net margin can be found on the profit and loss statements filed with the SEC. Total asset and shareholder's equity information can be found on the balance sheets filed with the SEC. All this information can be accessed through the SEC's EDGAR system at www.sec.gov/edgar.shtml.

CHAPTER ELEVEN

Working Capital and Operational Efficiency

 To make money, a business must manage its cash efficiently. A business that manages its cash efficiently won't need to tie up as much cash, which can lead to lower borrowing costs and the need for a smaller investment by the owners. In this chapter, we'll present a series of tools that can be used to measure the efficiency of a business in managing its cash.

Working Capital

Let's start our discussion of cash efficiency by talking about working capital. In order for a business to operate, it needs cash. This cash will either need to be obtained through the operation of the business, through borrowing, or from investment by the owners.

Almost all businesses will have some cash tied up in the business. This tied-up cash is known as working capital.

Working capital is defined as the difference between a business's current assets and current liabilities. As we discussed in Chapter 7, the current assets of a business include cash, accounts receivable, inventory, raw materials and work in process. The current liabilities of the business include the accounts payable and the current portion of any loans payable.

A manufacturing business will need cash to support the purchase of raw materials so it can produce inventory for shipment to customers, and a retail business will need cash to purchase inventory to stock its store. Any business with accounts receivable is in effect making a loan to its customers and will need cash to support its operations while awaiting payment from its customers. Conversely, a business with accounts payable is borrowing from its suppliers and will need to obtain less cash from other sources as a result.

Every business must make decisions such as how much inventory to produce or how much time to allow a customer to pay for a purchase. These decisions affect the working capital needed to operate the business.

A business that allows a customer a significant amount of time to pay will tie up more cash in the business than will one that gets paid sooner. Likewise, a business that produces and stores inventory ahead of customer demand will use more cash than one that produces products only when customer orders are in-hand. And businesses that operate efficiently will tie up less cash and be more profitable than ones that operate inefficiently.

Efficiency Ratios

For a business to make money, it must produce its products, sell these products (or sell its services), and collect the cash payment for these products or services. That is, it must convert its products and services into cash. Efficiency ratios can be used to help a business determine how quickly its products and services are being converted to cash.

Days in Inventory

Days in inventory measures the number of days inventory stays in the company before it's sold. In general, a business has to buy the inventory and, therefore, incurs a cost (such as using cash to pay for the inventory, or borrowing and paying interest to acquire the inventory) to bring that inventory onto the balance sheet. Therefore, the less time the inventory stays on the balance sheet, the less time, cash and other resources are tied up in inventory.

Here is the formula for days in inventory:

$$\text{Days in Inventory} = \frac{\text{Ending Inventory}}{\text{Cost of Goods Sold per Day}}$$

Ending inventory comes from the balance sheet. Note that many manufacturers include several categories of inventory on their balance sheets: finished inventory (also known as inventory), work in process, and raw materials. These categories are typically added together as inventory for the days in inventory calculation.

Cost of goods sold per day is computed as cost of goods sold from the annual profit and loss statement divided by 360. Note that we're using 360 as the number of days in the year rather than 365 or 366. This is a common convention in financial calculations. Financial analysts assume there are 360 days in each year, and that there are 30 days in each month. This allows for an easier month-to-month or year-to-year comparison of financial data. Throughout this book, we'll be following this convention for any "per day" calculations.

It is also possible to calculate a per day number using a monthly profit and loss statement. You would simply divide the cost of goods sold for the month by 30 rather than 360.

BY ANY OTHER NAME

Days in inventory is also known as *inventory conversion cycle*.

Collection Period

Collection period measures the time it takes customers to pay for the goods and services they purchase from a business. It's typical in many industries for customers to be granted 30, 60, 90 days or more to pay for the goods or services they purchase. Collection period measures how long it takes before customers pay.

The longer it takes for customers to pay, the more working capital a business will need to support its operations while waiting for payment. The lower the average collection period, the better. This indicates that customers are paying faster.

Here's the formula for collection period:

$$\text{Collection Period} = \frac{\text{Ending Accounts Receivable}}{\text{Revenue per Day}}$$

Ending accounts receivable can be found on the balance sheet. Revenue per day is computed as revenue from the annual profit and loss statement divided by 360. Collection period is expressed as a number of days.

BY ANY OTHER NAME

Collection period is also known as *days sales outstanding*. Collection period can also be calculated using average accounts receivable and may be known as *average collection period* and *average collection cycle*.

Payment Period

This ratio measures the number of days it takes the business to pay its bills. Payment period is a companion ratio to collection period. Collection period measures how fast the company gets paid, while payment period measures how fast the company pays its bills.

A business that gets paid slowly but pays its bills quickly could find itself needing to borrow more cash than a company that has a more balanced relationship between payables and receivables. On the other hand, a business with a long payment period will need less working capital since its suppliers have granted it favorable payment terms.

Here's the formula for payment period:

$$\text{Payment Period} = \frac{\textit{Ending Accounts Payable}}{\textit{Cost of Goods Sold per Day}}$$

Ending accounts payable can be found on the balance sheet. Cost of goods sold per day is computed as cost of goods sold from the annual profit and loss statement divided by 360. Payment period is expressed as a number of days.

BY ANY OTHER NAME

Payment period is also known as *days payables outstanding*. Payment period can also be calculated using average accounts payable and may be known as *average payment period* and *average payment cycle*.

Cash Conversion Cycle

The cash conversion cycle measures how many days it takes for a business to convert its products into cash. This ratio is calculated by summing the total number of days products are in inventory (days in inventory), plus the number of days it takes customers to pay for the products (collection period), less the number of days it takes the business to pay its suppliers (payment period).

Here's the formula for cash conversion cycle:

$$\text{Cash Conversion Cycle} = \text{Days in Inventory} + \text{Collection Period} - \text{Payment Period}$$

A business needs working capital so that it can operate until it's able to convert its products into cash. Shorter cash conversion cycles are preferred to longer cash conversion cycles as less money will be tied up in the business.

Inventory Turnover

Inventory turnover is a measure of how many times per year the inventory of a company turns over (i.e., is sold). The more often the inventory turns over, the better for the company. Since a business must use cash to purchase its inventory, the more frequently it's able to sell that inventory, the quicker cash is returned.

Here's the formula for inventory turnover:

$$\text{Inventory Turnover Ratio} = \frac{\text{Cost of Goods Sold}}{\text{Inventory}}$$

Managing the amount of inventory on the balance sheet and the inventory turnover ratio is what the "just-in-time" inventory practice the Japanese automakers are so famous for is all about. Rather than keep parts inventory on hand (and bear all the associated costs of this inventory), they get the inventory delivered a day or two before it's needed. This increases the inventory turnover, reduces the days in inventory, allows the company to have less cash tied up in inventory, and has the effect of enhancing the profitability of the company.

BY ANY OTHER NAME

Inventory turnover can also be computed using average inventory and can be known as *average inventory turnover*.

Asset Turnover

Asset turnover is a measure of how efficiently the business uses its assets to generate revenue. This ratio is calculated by dividing revenue by total assets and measures how much revenue is generated in relation to the assets of the business.

Here's the formula for asset turnover:

$$\text{Asset Ratio} = \frac{\text{Revenue}}{\text{Total Assets}}$$

The concept behind asset turnover is simple. Assets cost a business money to acquire. To be the most profitable, a business should use its assets as often as possible in the revenue-generation process.

For example, a manufacturing company that has constructed and equipped a factory might run the factory for two shifts rather than one shift. By running two shifts, the business can produce twice as many products using the same assets.

Likewise, a profitable restaurant will endeavor to have multiple customer seatings during the lunch or dinner rush so the use of the dining area is maximized. For instance, having three seatings allows the restaurant to serve three sets of customers per table at a meal rather than just one set.

BY ANY OTHER NAME

Asset turnover can also be computed using average assets and can be known as *average asset turnover*.

Efficiency at Boutique Handbags

Now let's look at the efficiency of our sample manufacturing company, Boutique Handbags. On the company's balance sheet (see page 167), note that Boutique Handbags has $80,000 in accounts receivable, as it allows customers to take up to 60 days to pay. Also note that the balance sheet includes $10,000 of finished inventory, $5,000 of work in process, and $2,000 of raw materials, for a total of $17,000 worth of inventory.

Boutique Handbags
Balance Sheet

Assets

Current Assets		
	Cash	$16,000
	Accounts Receivable	$80,000
	Inventory	$10,000
	Raw Materials	$2,000
	Work in Process	$5,000
Total Current Assets		**$113,000**
Plant, Property and Equipment		
	Equipment	$30,000
	Less: Accumulated Depreciation	($3,000)
Total Plant, Property and Equipment		**$27,000**
Total Assets		**$140,000**
Liabilities and Owners' Equity		
Liabilities		
Current Liabilities		
	Accounts Payable	$20,000
Total Current Liabilities		**$20,000**
Long-Term Liabilities		
	Bank Loan Payable	$68,000
Total Long-Term Liabilities		**$68,000**
Total Liabilities		**$88,000**
Owners' Equity		
	Owners' Investment	$40,000
	Retained Earnings	$12,000
Total Owners' Equity		**$52,000**
Total Liabilities and Owners' Equity		**$140,000**

Since the calculation of efficiency ratios involves the use of information from both the balance sheet and the profit and loss statement, let's also look at the profit and loss statement for Boutique Handbags (see page 168). Boutique earns a 50 percent gross margin from manufacturing its handbags. The handbags cost Boutique

$20 to manufacture, and Boutique sells them to retailers at a price of $40 each. If the business sold 12,000 handbags in one year, revenue would equal $480,000, and cost of goods sold would equal $240,000.

Boutique Handbags Profit and Loss Statement

Sales Activities	
Revenue	$480,000
Cost of Goods Sold	$240,000
Gross Profit	**$240,000**
Operating Expenses	
Selling Expenses	$18,000
General and Administrative Expenses	$126,000
Depreciation	$3,000
Total Operating Expenses	$147,000
Operating Profit	**$93,000**
Interest	$10,800
Profit before Taxes	**$82,200**
Income Taxes at 35%	$28,770
Net Profit	**$53,430**

Working Capital

Let's start with the calculation of working capital. The formula is current assets minus current liabilities. The current assets of Boutique Handbags are $113,000, and current liabilities are $20,000 ($113,000 - $20,000 = $93,000).

Boutique Handbags' working capital is $93,000. That is, the operation of Boutique Handbags requires that $93,000 be left in the business. This $93,000 will have come from either the owners' equity investment in the business, from borrowing, or from the profits of the business.

Now let's look at the efficiency of Boutique Handbags.

Days in Inventory

Days in inventory can be calculated by dividing ending inventory by cost of goods sold per day ($17,000/[$240,000/360] = 25.5). Boutique Handbags has 25.5 days in inventory.

Collection Period

Collection period can be calculated by dividing ending accounts receivable by revenue per day ($80,000/[$480,000/360] = 60). Boutique Handbags has a 60-day collection period.

Payment Period

Payment period can be calculated by dividing ending accounts payable by cost of goods sold per day ($20,000/[$240,000/360] = 30). Boutique Handbags has a 30-day payment period.

Cash Collection Cycle

Using our previous results, the cash collection cycle for Boutique Handbags can be calculated by adding days in inventory and collection period and subtracting payment period (25.5 days + 60 days − 30 days = 55.5 days).

Boutique Handbags as a 55.5-day cash collection cycle. In other words, on average, it takes Boutique Handbags 55.5 days to produce and sell its handbags and receive cash from the sale.

Inventory Turnover

The inventory turnover for Boutique Handbags can be calculated by dividing cost of goods sold by inventory ($240,000 /$17,000 = 14.1). Boutique Handbags turned over its inventory 14.1 times during the year.

Asset Turnover

The asset turnover for Boutique Handbags can be calculated by dividing Boutique's revenue by its total assets ($480,000/$140,000 = 4.2). Boutique Handbags turned over its assets 4.2 times during the year.

Analyzing Your Efficiency

Now that we've calculated all these ratios for Boutique Handbags, how do we tell if the business is operating efficiently, and if it is, can the efficiency of the business be improved? And if so, how?

We'll answer these questions by first examining how efficiency can be analyzed, and then in the following section by discussing how payment and collection periods can be managed, and conclude by reviewing the operating efficiency of Boutique Handbags.

Inventory

Let's start by looking at days in inventory and inventory turnover for different industries. Retail businesses that sell perishable goods or that sell large quantities of goods at low margins tend to have high inventory turnover and a low number of days in inventory. This group would include oil and gas retailers, food and beverage retailers, and can include discount department stores. These businesses make money by selling a large volume of products at low margins. Their inventory turnover rates can be as high as 15 times, although a range of 8 to 10 times is more typical. These businesses tend to have between 20 and 40 days of inventory in stock.

Retail businesses that sell nonperishable goods or that sell products at premium prices have lower inventory turnover and a higher number of days in inventory. These businesses tend to earn higher margins. This group would include clothing stores, home goods stores, and specialty stores, such as hardware or supply stores. The less perishable the inventory, the longer it can remain in stock at the retailers. Inventory turnover rates for this group of businesses are typically 2 to 4 times. There are examples of auto parts retailers and other specialty retailers in this group that turn over their inventory less than 2 times in a year. Days in inventory for this group typically ranges from between 80 to 120 days.

An EFFICIENT business needs less cash to operate than an INEFFICIENT business.

We see a similar pattern with manufacturers. Manufacturers of pharmaceuticals and medical, scientific and specialty equipment tend to have low inventory turnover and a large number of days in inventory. These manufacturers sell high-margin products. Inventory turnover tends to be between 2 to 5 times, and days in inventory typically ranges from 100 to 150 days.

Manufacturers of consumer goods have a higher inventory turnover and a smaller number of days in inventory. The inventory turnover for consumer goods manufacturers ranges from 4 to 8 times, and days in inventory ranges from 45 to 80 days.

Service businesses typically don't have inventory, so inventory turnover and days in inventory don't affect the efficiency of a service business.

The chart on page 172 details inventory turnover rates and days in inventory for various types of businesses.

Inventory Turnover by Business Type

	Inventory Turnover	Days in Inventory
Retail Businesses		
Low Margin – High Volume	8 to 10 times	20 to 40 days
Food and beverage retailers		
Oil and gas retailers		
Discount department stores		
High Margin – Low Volume	2 to 4 times	80 to 120 days
Clothing stores		
Home goods stores		
Specialty stores		
Manufacturing Businesses		
Consumer products manufacturers	4 to 8 times	45 to 80 days
Clothing		
Home goods		
Household products		
Specialty Manufacturers	2 to 5 times	100 to 150 days
Pharmaceuticals		
Medical and scientific equipment		

Collection And Payment

Now let's look at the collection period for different types of businesses. Retail businesses tend to be paid very quickly. Customers either pay with cash received at the time of sale, or with checks or credit and debit cards, where the business receives payment within a few days. Retail businesses as a group have minimal accounts receivable. As a result, the collection period for most retail businesses is under 10 days.

Accounts receivable can be a significant item for a manufacturer. The collection period for manufacturers of consumer products typically ranges from 25 to 45 days. Consumer product manufacturers tend to allow the retailer credit terms that require payment in 30 to 60 days.

The collection period for manufacturers of medical, scientific and specialty equipment ranges from 50 to 80 days, reflective of credit terms that require the customer to pay in 60 to 90 days.

For service businesses, the collection period varies based on the type of business and whether a third party is paying the bill. Service businesses focused on the individual customer, such as plumbing or electrical services, tend to require payment at the time of service, so their collection period looks much like the collection period of a retail business.

> **Your ability to manage PAYMENT and COLLECTION terms greatly depends on the industry you're in and your relative position in that INDUSTRY.**

Service businesses that provide services to other businesses (e.g., advertising, marketing, consulting) are able to negotiate payment terms in their contracts, may receive periodic payments during the term of the contract, and receive final payment upon the completion of the job. In these instances, the collection cycle may be 30 to 90 days.

The collection cycle for medical practitioners can exceed 90 days. Medical practitioners typically treat patients and then receive payment for these treatments from government or private insurance programs. The time between treatment and reimbursement by the insurance plan can be 90 to 180 days, or longer in some instances.

Payment periods also vary by type of business. Food and beverage retailers and oil and gas retailers tend to pay the fastest. The payment period for this group of retailers is between 20 and 30 days. Discount department stores and other higher-volume retailers have payment periods between 25 and 35 days, while the payment period for specialty and lower-volume retailers tends to be between 30 and 60 days.

The payment period for manufacturers of consumer goods ranges from 30 to 60 days, while the payment period for manufacturers of medical, scientific and specialty equipment ranges from 60 to 90 days.

The chart below summarizes the collection and payment periods by business type.

Collection and Payment Periods by Business Type

	Collection Period	Payment Period
Retail Businesses		
Low margin – High volume	Under 10 days	20 to 30 days
High margin – Low volume	Under 10 days	30 to 60 days
Manufacturing Businesses		
Consumer products	25 to 45 days	30 to 60 days
Specialty manufacturers	50 to 80 days	60 to 90 days
Service Businesses		
Consumer services	Under 10 days	30 days
Business services	30 to 90 days	30 to 60 days
Medical services	90 to 180 days	30 to 60 days

Cash Conversion Cycle

Low-margin, high-volume businesses tend to have the shortest cash conversion cycles, while high-margin, low-volume businesses tend to have longer cash conversion cycles.

Food and beverage retailers, oil and gas retailers, and discount department stores have cash conversion cycles that are often under 15 days. The cash conversion cycle for consumer product and clothing retailers ranges from 45 to 75 days.

Manufacturers of consumer products have cash conversion cycles that can range from 45 to 75 days, while the cash conversion cycle of medical, scientific, and specialty manufacturers can also range from 45 to 75 days, although in some instances it may take more than 90 days.

The cash conversion cycle for service businesses varies greatly depending on the type of services provided and the payment practices in the industry. Businesses providing services directly to consumers can have a cash conversion cycle of under 10 days, while those providing services to other businesses might have a cash conversion cycle of 30 to 60 days. A medical practice might have a cash conversion cycle of three to six months as it awaits payments from insurance companies.

The chart below shows the cash conversion cycle by business type.

Cash Conversion Cycle by Business Type

	Cash Conversion Cycle
Retail Businesses	
Low margin – High volume	Under 15 days
High margin – Low volume	45 to 75 days
Manufacturing Businesses	
Consumer products	45 to 75 days
Specialty manufacturers	45 to 75 days
Service Businesses	
Consumer services	Under 10 days
Business services	30 to 60 days
Medical services	90 to 180 days

Managing Collection and Payment Periods

Collection and payment periods can be one of the most difficult areas for a business to manage.

Traditional finance textbooks often include the advice that to improve your cash collection cycle you should use strategies where you try to reduce the number of days it takes to collect your accounts receivable (that is, reduce your collection period), and you should strive to increase the number of days it takes to pay your accounts payable (that is, increase your payment period).

As a business owner or manager, you should be aware of the credit terms extended to customers and where the collection period stands relative to these credit terms. For instance, if your business extends credit terms that allow customers 30 days to pay, and the collection period is 40 days, something is wrong. Your customers aren't paying you in a timely fashion. They're taking an extra 10 days to make their payments. You should clearly step up your collection activities in an effort to get paid on time.

Likewise, if your suppliers extend credit terms that allow 60 days to pay, and your payment period is 45 days, you may be paying your bills too fast and should consider slowing your payments to match the terms offered by the suppliers.

Additionally, a business owner or manager should be aware of the payment and collection periods typical for their industry and make certain that his/her business is achieving payment and collection periods that are at least as good as those that are typical for the industry.

However, managing your payment and collection periods isn't always as easy as described in the finance textbooks. Your ability to manage payment and collection terms greatly depends on the industry you're in and your relative position in that industry.

A small entrepreneurial business will often find it very difficult, if not impossible, to dictate payment terms to a large, established customer or supplier. In order to sell to this customer, or purchase from this supplier, the business will need to adhere to the existing payment terms.

For instance, if a small manufacturing business were to sell products to some large retailers, such as Wal-Mart, Target or Costco, and these retailers have established payment periods of 60 days, it would most likely be impossible for the small manufacturer to dictate payment terms different than 60 days. As much as the manufacturer might like to be paid in 30 days, it's highly unlikely that a large customer will accommodate such payment terms.

Small manufacturers face this problem in dealing with large customers or suppliers, small retailers have this problem when purchasing inventory from established manufacturers or wholesalers, and small service businesses have this problem when providing services to large clients. Medical practices face this problem all the time when waiting for payment from government-sponsored and private insurance programs.

A business is much more likely to be able to negotiate payment and collection terms when the negotiations are with a business of similar size or relative position in the industry.

To the extent possible, you should try to decrease your collection period and increase your payment period to reduce your cash conversion cycle. However, your ability to do this is very much dependent on the size of your customers or suppliers and the established practices of the industry.

Is Boutique Handbags Efficient?

Now that we've looked at efficiency ratios for different types of businesses and analyzed some of the drivers of these ratios, let's go back to our example of Boutique Handbags. Is Boutique Handbags efficient?

Boutique Handbags turns over its inventory 14.1 times per year and has 25.5 days in inventory. In comparison to the typical manufacturer, Boutique Handbags is very efficient. Inventory turnover for most manufacturers is below 10 times, and Boutique Handbags is at 14.1 times. Days in inventory for many manufacturers is 45 days or more, and Boutique Handbags has only 25.5 days in inventory.

By having a lower number of days in inventory than is the norm, Boutique Handbags is either operating very efficiently (perhaps effectively using a just-in-time inventory process), or is at risk of product shortages should demand increase or problems occur in the production cycle.

A business needs WORKING CAPITAL so that it can operate until it's able to CONVERT its products into cash.

Boutique Handbags has a collection period of 60 days and a payment period of 30 days. The business is paying its bills in 30 days, and getting paid by its customers in 60 days. In comparison to the typical consumer products manufacturer, Boutique Handbags is less efficient in collecting payments from its customers. Boutique Handbags has a collection period of 60 days, while many other manufacturers get paid in 25 to 45 days. Boutique Handbags could improve its cash collection cycle by changing its credit terms to require payment in 30 or 45 days, but this may prove difficult since its customers include high-end department stores that are generally able to dictate the payment period to suppliers such as Boutique Handbags.

If Boutique Handbags were able to reduce its collection period, this would have the effect of reducing accounts receivables, which in turn would reduce the amount of working capital in the business. If Boutique reduced its collection period from 60 days to 45 days, it could reduce accounts receivable from $80,000 to $60,000, freeing up $20,000 of working capital that could be used to reduce bank borrowing or used to repay the owners.

Boutique's payment period is 30 days, which is within the 30- to 60-day range typical for other manufacturers. This 30-day payment period is at the low end of the typical range. This may indicate an opportunity to find different suppliers who will allow a longer payment period, or it may indicate that Boutique is willing to pay its suppliers a bit sooner in exchange for the supplier selling raw materials with a just-in-time inventory process.

Overall, the cash collection cycle at Boutique Handbags is 55.5 days. A 55.5-day cash collection cycle is very consistent with the 45- to 75-day cash collection cycle found in many consumer product manufacturing companies. In this regard, while there are opportunities to improve efficiency, Boutique Handbags appears to be as efficient as similar manufacturers.

As you can see, an efficient business needs less cash to operate than an inefficient business. Efficiency ratios play a critical role in measuring how efficiently a business is being managed. But using your cash efficiently is just one key to creating and managing a profitable business. A business must also have sufficient cash available to pay its bills, which is the topic of our next chapter.

CHAPTER TWELVE

Can You Pay Your Bills?

As we have emphasized several times in earlier chapters, it's important that a business has cash, since a business must pay its bills with cash. A business that doesn't have the cash to pay its bills won't be able to continue to operate.

Liquidity Ratios

In this chapter, we'll discuss two liquidity ratios that can be used to measure the ability of the business to pay its upcoming bills: current ratio and quick ratio.

Current Ratio

In Chapter 7, we defined current assets as assets that are already in cash, or that the business can expect to convert to cash within one year. In addition to cash, current assets include the business's accounts receivable and inventory.

We also defined current liabilities as the debts of the business that must be paid within the next year. The key components of current liabilities are the business's accounts payable and any loan payments due within the next year. Current liabilities can also include payroll taxes due and any lease payments the business must make.

The current ratio is calculated by dividing current assets by current liabilities:

$$\textbf{\textit{Current Ratio}} = \frac{\textbf{\textit{Current Assets}}}{\textbf{\textit{Current Liabilities}}}$$

If current assets exceed current liabilities, the current ratio will be greater than 1.0. A current ratio greater than 1.0 indicates that the business has sufficient assets to pay its bills over the next year. If the current ratio is less than 1.0, this indicates the business doesn't have sufficient current assets to pay its bills in the coming year.

Quick Ratio

The chief criticism of the current ratio as a measure of a business's ability to pay its bills is that the calculation assumes all the current assets of the business will be turned into cash within the next year and available to pay current liabilities.

Cash assets are certainly available to pay bills. In almost all instances, accounts receivable will be collected within the next year. But what about inventory? In order to convert inventory to cash, the business must first sell the inventory and collect any accounts receivable that result from these sales.

In many instances, the business will be able to complete this process and convert its inventory into cash. In other cases, if the inventory has been slow to sell, has become technologically obsolete, or has spoiled or been damaged, converting this inventory into cash may be more difficult. The process may take longer, or prices may have to be discounted to make the sale.

As a result of these criticisms, there's often a need to look at a ratio that doesn't include inventory. Here is where the quick ratio comes in.

The quick ratio measures the ability of a business to pay its bills by comparing the assets of the business that can be readily turned into cash (cash, accounts receivable, but not inventory) against current liabilities.

Here's the formula for the quick ratio:

$$\textbf{Quick Ratio} = \frac{\textbf{Current Assets} - \textbf{Inventory}}{\textbf{Current Liabilities}}$$

A quick ratio greater than 1.0 indicates that a business has sufficient cash assets to pay its bills over the coming year. A quick ratio less than 1.0 indicates that a business may be short of cash during the coming year.

BY ANY OTHER NAME

The quick ratio is also known as the *acid test*.

One-Year Time Horizon

Since the ability of a business to pay its bills is critical to its survival, one consideration when using a current ratio or quick ratio is the one-year time horizon. The use of one year as the appropriate time horizon is very much dependent on the business's cash collection cycle.

In order for a business to have sufficient cash to pay its bills, it's very important that the timing of the receipt of cash coincides with the bills to be paid, or that the business otherwise has sufficient cash on hand to pay the bills as they come due.

Typical payment periods are 30 to 60 days, and typical collection periods are 30 to 90 days. To the extent that a business has a long cash conversion cycle, where the collection period is significantly longer than the payment period, a business might have current ratios and quick ratios that are above 1.0, and yet not have the cash available to pay its bills as they come due.

In evaluating the ability of your business to pay its bills, you may consider using modified versions of the current ratio or quick ratio, where you look at the ability of your business to pay its bills during the next three months, or even during the next month.

One of the things we found in researching this book is that many businesses also evaluate their ability to pay their bills over the next few months. In doing so, they're able to make sure they have sufficient cash to continue operating the business.

The one-year time horizon for the current ratio and the quick ratio result from some accounting rules used in creating the balance sheet. If these rules are inconsistent with your need to manage your business to make money, there's no reason you can't modify these calculations a bit and review your business's ability to pay its bills over the next month or quarter.

Liquidity at Bonnie's Beachwear

Let's look at the liquidity ratios for our sample retail company, Bonnie's Beachwear.

After three months of operations, the balance sheet for Bonnie's Beachwear (on page 185) shows $47,400 of current assets, consisting of $20,400 in cash and $27,000 in inventory. Current liabilities are $18,000 in accounts payable.

Bonnie's Beachwear Balance Sheet
After 3 Months of Operations

Assets	
Current Assets	
Cash	$20,400
Inventory	$27,000
Total Current Assets	**$47,400**
Plant, Property and Equipment	
Equipment	$10,000
Less: Accumulated Depreciation	($600)
Furniture and Fixtures	$40,000
Less: Accumulated Depreciation	($2,400)
Total Plant, Property and Equipment	**$47,000**
Total Assets	**$94,400**
Liabilities and Owners' Equity	
Liabilities	
Current Liabilities	
Accounts Payable	$18,000
Total Current Liabilities	**$18,000**
Long-Term Liabilities	
Bank Loan Payable	$30,000
Total Long-Term Liabilities	**$30,000**
Total Liabilities	**$48,000**
Owners' Equity	
Owners' Investment	$30,000
Retained Earnings	$16,400
Total Owners' Equity	**$46,400**
Total Liabilities and Owners' Equity	**$94,400**

The current ratio for Bonnie's Beachwear is 2.6 ($47,000/$18,000 = 2.6). This indicates that the business has 2.6 times more current assets than current liabilities and should have no problem paying its bills within the next year.

The quick ratio for Bonnie's Beachwear is 1.1 ($20,400/$18,000 = 1.1). This indicates that the business has 1.1 times more cash assets than current liabilities and should have no problem paying its bills within the next year.

Understanding Liquidity Ratios

As with profitability and efficiency ratios, liquidity ratios vary by the type of business and by the operating strategies of the business.

Businesses such as food and beverage retailers, oil and gas retailers, and discount department stores have the lowest current ratios. The current ratio for these businesses is often at or under 1.0. These same businesses have a very quick cash conversion cycle, and their accounts payable tend to be for inventory purchases that will be converted to cash very quickly.

> **LIQUIDITY RATIOS vary by type of business and by the operating strategies of the BUSINESS.**

The current ratio for consumer goods manufacturers is typically between 1.0 and 1.5. These businesses tend to have more inventory, resulting in more current assets, and a higher current ratio. When the effect of the inventory is removed, the consumer-goods manufacturers have quick ratios between 0.7 and 1.0.

Current ratios for medical, scientific, and specialty manufacturers range from 1.5 to 2.5, while quick ratios for this group of manufacturers range from 1.3 to 2.2.

The current and quick ratios for retailers can vary based on the retailer's operating strategy. Retailers who focus on high-end customers often have the highest ratios. The current ratio for high-margin, low-volume retailers is often 2.0 or above, while quick ratios between 1.0 and 1.5 are common. Retailers who focus on middle-class customers have current ratios between 1.0 and 2.5, and have quick ratios that are near 1.0.

The current ratio for Bonnie's Beachwear was 2.6, and the quick ratio was 1.1. Bonnie's business focus is on higher-end customers, so the ratios are consistent with the industry's ratios for high-end retail businesses.

Liquidity ratios provide a means to assess a business's capacity to pay its bills. A company's ability to pay its bills is important not only to the owners and managers of the business but also to its lenders.

CHAPTER THIRTEEN

Can You Pay the Bank?

When a business sets out to acquire assets to be used in its production processes, it has three options to pay for these assets:

1. It can use the profits earned by the business.
2. It can use an equity investment by the owner.
3. It can borrow the money from a bank or other lending institution.

Borrowing often allows a business to grow more quickly than if it had to rely on profits or additional owners' equity investment for growth. When a new business is starting out, the money the owner has to invest can be limited and the venture isn't yet earning profits, so borrowing may be the only source of money available to support growth.

Leverage Ratios

In the financial world, leverage refers to the borrowings done by a company in an attempt to grow the business and enhance the returns to the owners and other investors.

When a lender provides a loan to a business, it will often look at its leverage ratios to determine if the loan can be repaid. Lenders use leverage ratios to compare the level of debt in a business and to measure the ability of a business to repay that debt. The most common leverage ratios are the debt to equity ratio, the interest coverage ratio and the fixed payment coverage ratio. We'll start by reviewing the debt to equity ratio.

Debt to Equity Ratio

How quickly a business chooses to grow and how much debt it decides take on are often individual decisions made by each business. Some businesses may use moderate amounts of debt, others may borrow very heavily, and some may use no debt at all.

The debt to equity ratio measures the amount of debt a company has in comparison to the amount of equity invested in the company.

Here's the formula for the debt to equity ratio:

$$\textbf{Debt to Equity} = \frac{\textbf{Total Liabilities}}{\textbf{Owners' Equity}}$$

A debt to equity ratio of 1.0 means a business has one dollar of debt for every dollar the owners have invested. Half the assets in the business have been acquired using the owners' money, and half have been acquired using borrowed money.

A debt to equity ratio in excess of 1.0 means that the business has borrowed more money than the owners have invested. It's not uncommon for businesses to borrow two or three times more than their owners' investment. A debt to equity ratio below 1.0 means that the owners have invested more than the business has borrowed.

A business's debt to equity ratio is a very important ratio to bankers and other lenders, as it tells the banker how leveraged the business is. Banks in general tend to be very conservative when they make loans to businesses, particularly small or startup businesses. The key criteria are the business's ability to repay the loan from its operating activities or from its assets, if the business doesn't earn enough from operating activities.

A low debt to equity ratio indicates a business without much other debt. Bankers like this. This means the business should be able to earn enough money to repay the loan, and if it doesn't earn enough, it should be able to sell some assets. Bankers don't like high debt to equity ratios. A high debt to equity ratio indicates a business might have difficulty earning enough to repay the loan.

Interest Coverage Ratio

In addition to the debt to equity ratio, bankers also use the interest coverage ratio to help them make lending decisions.

The interest coverage ratio is calculated by dividing operating profit by interest payments:

$$\textit{Interest Coverage} = \frac{\textit{Operating Profit}}{\textit{Interest Payments}}$$

When a business borrows money, the money must be repaid, so a business that borrows money must earn sufficient profits to repay its debts. The interest coverage ratio measures the ability of a business to earn the money needed to pay the interest on its borrowings.

The interest coverage ratio shows the ratio of earnings before interest and taxes (aka operating profit) to annual interest costs. That is, it measures how many times larger the earnings before interest and taxes are than the annual interest costs. This is a measure of the company's ability to pay the interest costs.

A ratio below 1.0 indicates that the company doesn't have sufficient earnings before interest and taxes to pay its interest costs and indicates that the company could soon be out of business unless it finds some way to pay the interest when it comes due.

Bankers typically like to see an interest coverage ratio of 2.0 or greater. This means the company has sufficient earnings before interest and taxes (plus some extra) to pay its annual interest costs. Bankers like to see the operating profit in excess of interest costs so the company has some extra funds should profits be lower than expected.

Fixed Payment Coverage Ratio

There's one other ratio bankers use to help them make lending decisions: the fixed payment coverage ratio.

Many businesses today lease equipment rather than purchase it. The lease payments are an obligation of the company, but their existence isn't reflected in the interest coverage ratio. The interest coverage ratio might present an inaccurate picture of the company if much of the equipment is leased. Therefore, the fixed payment coverage ratio was developed to allow the comparison of companies that purchase their equipment with those that lease their equipment.

The fixed payment coverage ratio measures the ability of the company to generate sufficient earnings to meet their fixed payment liabilities.

The fixed payment coverage ratio is calculated as follows:

$$\text{Fixed Payment Coverage Ratio} = \frac{\text{Operating Profit} + \text{Asset Lease Payments}}{\text{Interest} + \text{Principal} + \text{Asset Lease Payments}}$$

This ratio is a bit more complicated than some of the others we've discussed, and this complication results from the accounting rules that went into creating the profit and loss statement.

Under accounting rules, asset lease payments are deducted as an expense when calculating operating profit, but interest payments are not. Both are fixed payments the business must make, but they're treated differently by accountants.

To determine whether the business is generating a sufficient profit to make its asset lease payments and its interest payments, we need to know what the operating profit is before the asset lease payments, so we add the asset lease payments back into the operating profit. This is done in the numerator portion of the fixed payment coverage ratio equation above. This gives us the profit of the business before interest payments and before asset lease payments.

The denominator part of the equation is the fixed lease and debt payments the business has to make. This includes interest payments, principal payments, and asset lease payments.

We can then calculate the fixed payment coverage ratio by dividing the operating profit the business has available for fixed payments by the fixed payments the business needs to make. If the ratio is greater than 1.0, the business has sufficient profits to make its fixed payments. If the ratio is less than 1.0, the business isn't earning sufficient profits to make the required fixed payments.

As in the case of the interest coverage ratio, bankers like to see fixed payment coverage ratios of 2.0 or greater so the business has a cushion should profits be lower than expected.

Leverage at Uptown Chiropractic

Now let's look at the leverage ratios for our service company, Uptown Chiropractic. Uptown Chiropractic is unique among our sample companies in that it has leased its medical equipment and has borrowed some funds for working capital from a bank.

Rather than purchase the medical treatment equipment used in its offices, the business has chosen to lease this equipment. A monthly leasing expense of $4,500 appears as a general and administrative expense on the business's profit and loss statement (see page 194). Because the equipment is leased and therefore not owned by Uptown Chiropractic, it doesn't appear on the business's balance sheet (see page 195).

Uptown Chiropractic
Profit and Loss Statement

Sales Activities	
Revenue	$24,000
Cost of Services	$11,500
Gross Profit	**$12,500**
Operating Expenses	
General and Administrative	
Rent	$2,000
Utilities	$1,000
Equipment Lease	$4,500
Bookkeeper/Billing Clerk	$1,500
Licenses, Certifications, Training	$500
Accounting, Payroll and Legal Services	$500
Total General and Administrative	**$10,000**
Depreciation	$83
Total Operating Expenses	**$10,083**
Operating Profit	**$2,417**
Interest	$400
Profit before Taxes	**$2,017**
Income Taxes @ 35%	$706
Net Profit	**$1,311**

Uptown Chiropractic
Balance Sheet

Assets	
Current Assets	
Cash	$9,500
Accounts Receivable	$49,500
Inventory	$0
Total Current Assets	**$59,000**
Plant, Property and Equipment	
Equipment	$10,000
Less: Accumulated Depreciation	($500)
Total Plant, Property and Equipment	**$9,500**
Total Assets	**$68,500**
Liabilities and Owners' Equity	
Liabilities	
Current Liabilities	
Accounts Payable	$500
Total Current Liabilities	**$500**
Long-Term Liabilities	
Loan from Bank	$40,000
Total Long-Term Liabilities	**$40,000**
Total Liabilities	**$40,500**
Owners' Equity	
Owners' Investment	$20,000
Retained Earnings	$8,000
Total Owners' Equity	**$28,000**
Total Liabilities and Owners' Equity	**$68,500**

As a medical business, Uptown Chiropractic often must wait 120 days between the time of treatment and when it gets reimbursed by the patient's insurance company. This creates a need for a significant amount of working capital.

If we subtract current liabilities from current assets, we see that Uptown Chiropractic's working capital is $58,500. Looking further at the balance sheet, we see that the business has been funded using a $40,000 loan from the bank, a $20,000 investment by the owner, and with $8,000 of retained earnings.

The debt to equity ratio for Uptown Chiropractic is 1.45 ($40,500/$28,000 = 1.45). For every dollar of equity, the business has $1.45 in debt.

Looking at the profit and loss statement, we see that Uptown Chiropractic made an operating profit of $2,417 for the month and paid $400 in interest.

The interest coverage ratio for Uptown Chiropractic is 6.04 ($2,417/$400 = 6.04). The profits of the business were more than 6 times the required monthly interest costs. At this level of profits, the business shouldn't have difficulty making its interest payments.

Lenders use LEVERAGE RATIOS... to measure the ability of a business to REPAY that debt.

Now let's look at Uptown Chiropractic's fixed payment coverage ratio. The most significant operating expense for Uptown Chiropractic is the $4,500 per month lease payment for its treatment equipment.

In computing the fixed payment coverage ratio, we have to add this lease payment back into the operating expenses. The numerator for the fixed payment coverage ratio becomes operating profit plus lease payments ($2,417 + $4,500 = $6,917). The denominator for the equation includes the monthly fixed payments of the business, interest and the lease payments ($400 + $4,500 = $4,900).

The fixed payment coverage ratio for Uptown Chiropractic is 1.41 ($6,917/$4,900 = 1.41). The operating profits of the business (after adjusting for asset lease payments) are 1.41 times the monthly fixed payments. The business has sufficient profits to pay its monthly fixed payments, although the margin of safety isn't as high as its bankers would prefer.

Industry Leverage Ratios

Debt to equity ratios, interest coverage ratios, and fixed payment coverage ratios vary among businesses, even within the same industry.

Businesses that are more profitable tend to have lower debt to equity ratios. These businesses are able to use the profits from their operations to fuel their growth. Companies that are less profitable are more likely to use debt to grow.

For example, high-end and consumer product retailers tend to have debt to equity ratios between 0.5 and 0.7. These businesses aren't using significant debt. Food and beverage retailers, oil and gas retailers, and discount department stores tend to have debt to equity ratios between 1.0 and 1.5.

For manufacturers, the debt to equity ratio often depends on the capital intensity of the manufacturing process. Manufacturers of pharmaceuticals, and medical, scientific and specialty equipment tend to use more intellectual than physical capital to produce their products, so their debt to equity ratio tends to be lower. The debt to equity ratio for this type of company is generally below 1.0, often ranging from 0.4 to 0.7.

The manufacturing process for consumer products and household products is more capital intensive as more machinery and equipment is needed for the production process. The debt to equity ratio for these manufacturers can range from 1.0 to 2.0, with some manufacturers having debt to equity ratios of 4.0 or more.

Uptown Chiropractic has a debt to equity ratio of 1.45. This ratio appears to be a bit higher than for some of the industries described above. However, Uptown Chiropractic is in a unique business, where a very long collection period is typical, and to pay the bills while waiting for reimbursement from the insurance companies, it's necessary to have a significant amount of working capital. For many medical practices, this working capital must be obtained by borrowing.

CHAPTER FOURTEEN

Measuring Growth

It's critical that business owners and managers keep abreast of the changes occurring in their financial statements from period to period. In that respect, one of the most valuable things a business can do is compare the values on the cash flow statement, profit and loss statement, and balance sheet with the values from prior periods.

In this chapter, we'll discuss how to measure the growth of a business, and why measuring and managing growth is important to keeping a company profitable.

Understanding Growth Rates

Growth rates are a key tool that can be used to compare relative changes among the various sections in a financial statement and tell you which areas of the business are growing, which are stable, and which are falling. For instance, in a growing business, you might compare the growth rates of revenue and gross profit with that of operating expenses. As a business grows, operating expenses should be increasing at a slower rate than the revenue and gross profit. When this happens, the business becomes more profitable. If operating expenses are growing faster than revenue and gross profit, the business is becoming less profitable. An analysis of growth rates can tell you where and why your business is becoming more or less profitable.

The basic formula for a growth rate is:

$$\text{Growth Rate} = \frac{\text{Ending Value} - \text{Beginning Value}}{\text{Beginning Value}}$$

This formula can be applied to any of the values on a business's financial statements. For instance, the revenue growth rate can be calculated as:

$$\text{Revenue Growth Rate} = \frac{\text{Ending Revenue} - \text{Beginning Revenue}}{\text{Beginning Revenue}}$$

Growth Rates at Bonnie's Beachwear

To see how growth rates work, let's look at Bonnie's Beachwear over a three-month period. We'll compare two profit and loss statements for Bonnie's Beachwear as well as the store's beginning and ending balance sheet.

Analyzing Bonnie's Profit and Loss Statements

In earlier chapters, we presented the profit and loss statement for Bonnie's Beachwear, and assumed the business made 1,000 sales per month at an average price of $50. In this scenario, Bonnie's Beachwear had $50,000 in revenue, a cost of goods sold of $18,000, and $22,833 in operating expenses, including $10,000 for the sales staff's salaries, and $2,000 in advertising expenses. The business also earned a profit of $32,000, an operating profit of $9,167, and a net profit of $5,471. These results for this scenario are shown in the March 2010 column of the profit and loss statement for Bonnie's Beachwear (see page 202).

Let's fast forward three months and look at the profit and loss statement for June 2010. In April 2010, Bonnie decided she wanted to grow the sales of the business. To accomplish this, Bonnie decided to increase the advertising expenditures of the business from $2,000 per month to $4,000 per month. The additional advertising money was targeted at tourists staying in local hotels and included fliers in hotel welcome packets and advertising on guest information channels broadcast on in-room televisions.

> **GROWTH RATES are a key tool that can...**
> **tell you which areas of the BUSINESS**
> **are GROWING, which are STABLE,**
> **and which are FALLING.**

This increased advertising succeeded in boosting Bonnie's monthly sales from 1,000 units per month to 1,200 units per month.

As a result of this increase, Bonnie had to keep additional sales staff on at peak hours, which translated to an increase in sales staff salaries from $10,000 per month to $11,000.

In this scenario, Bonnie's Beachwear has $60,000 in revenue, a cost of goods sold of $21,600, and operating expenses of $25,833. The results for Bonnie's Beachwear at this higher level of sales are presented in the June 2010 column of the profit and loss statement for Bonnie's Beachwear (see page 202).

Bonnie's Beachwear Profit and Loss Statement	March 2010	June 2010	Growth Rates
Sales Activities			
Revenue	$50,000	$60,000	**20%**
Cost of Goods Sold	$18,000	$21,600	**20%**
Gross Profit	**$32,000**	**$38,400**	**20%**
Operating Expenses			
Selling Expenses			
Advertising	$2,000	$4,000	**100%**
Sales Staff Salary	$10,000	$11,000	**10%**
General and Administrative			
Rent	$3,000	$3,000	
Utilities	$1,500	$1,500	
Owners' Salary	$4,500	$4,500	
Accounting, Payroll and Legal	$1,000	$1,000	
Depreciation	$833	$833	
Total Operating Expenses	$22,833	$25,833	**13%**
Operating Profit	**$9,167**	**$12,567**	**37%**
Interest	$750	$750	
Profit Before Taxes	**$8,417**	**$11,817**	
Income Taxes @ 35%	$2,946	$4,136	
Net Profit	**$5,471**	**$7,681**	**40%**

Now let's look at the growth for the items on Bonnie's profit and loss statement. These are presented in the growth rate column above.

Revenue increased from $50,000 to $60,000. This is a 20 percent growth rate ([$60,000 - $50,000]/$50,000 = 20%).

Cost of goods sold also increased by 20 percent, from $18,000 to $21,600 ([$21,600 - $18,000]/$18,000] = 20%), as did gross profit, which grew from $32,000 to $38,400.

As a result of the changes to the advertising budget and the extra time required from the sales staff, total operating expenses increased 13 percent, from $22,833 to $25,833. However, not all operating expenses rose. The advertising expense increased 100 percent, from $2,000 to $4,000, and the sales staff salary expense grew 10 percent, from $10,000 to $11,000 per month. The other operating expenses did not increase.

Operating profit at Bonnie's Beachwear increased 37 percent, from $9,167 to $12,567, and net profit grew 40 percent, from $5,471 to $7,681.

This analysis of Bonnie's profit and loss statement demonstrates why a profitable business will watch its growth rates. In our example, Bonnie's Beachwear doubled the business's advertising spending and generated a 20 percent increase in revenue.

Note that this 20 percent increase in revenue doesn't translate to a 20 percent growth in profits. Both operating profit and net profit increased by *more* than 20 percent. There are several reasons for this.

If OPERATING EXPENSES are growing faster than revenue and gross profit, the business will be LESS PROFITABLE.

First, operating expenses didn't grow as fast as revenue and cost of goods sold. When a business is able to increase gross profit without a proportionate increase in operating expenses, it will be more profitable. In management speak, this is known as scalability or economies of scale. Revenue and gross profit increase, but operating expenses remain relatively constant, so most of the increased revenue is captured as profit rather than paid as operating expenses.

Note that the opposite of this is true as well: If operating expenses are growing faster than revenue and gross profit, the business will be less profitable, as revenue is being used to pay operating expenses rather than being captured as profit.

In the case of Bonnie's Beachwear, only the operating expenses associated with selling activities (advertising and staff salaries) increased with the growth in sales. The business's general and administrative expenses (rent, utilities, the owner's salary, and accounting, payroll and legal services) didn't increase with the growth in sales. This is consistent with our expectations. We wouldn't have really expected Bonnie's general and administrative expenses to have increased. The store size didn't change, so there's no reason to expect a change in rent. Bonnie's is open the same number of hours, so there wouldn't be a change in the utilities expense. The owner didn't get a raise, and the only change for the accountants is that the numbers in the calculations are slightly larger.

The second reason Bonnie's profits grew more than the 20 percent increase in revenue and gross profit is because the interest expenses didn't rise as a result of the boost in sales volume. The business was already profitable and generating a positive cash flow, so growing the business didn't require any additional borrowing to fund its growth.

Again, this isn't always the case. If Bonnie's didn't have sufficient cash flow to increase its inventory levels or to pay its higher operating expenses, the business might have had to borrow in order to fund the growth, and its interest expenses would have been more, decreasing the net profit growth rate.

Analyzing Bonnie's Balance Sheet

Let's look at the effect this increase in sales volume has had on the balance sheet of Bonnie's Beachwear. Follow along on page 205, where you'll find the balance sheets for March 2010, when sales were 1,000 units per month, and for June 2010, when sales increased to 1,200 units per month.

Bonnie's Beachwear Balance Sheet	End March 2010	End June 2010	Growth Rates
Assets			
Current Assets			
Cash	$20,400	$42,000	**106%**
Inventory	$27,000	$32,400	**20%**
Total Current Assets	**$47,400**	**$74,400**	**57%**
Plant, Property and Equipment			
Equipment	$10,000	$10,000	
Less: Accumulated Depreciation	($600)	($1,200)	
Furniture and Fixtures	$40,000	$40,000	
Less: Accumulated Depreciation	($2,400)	($4,800)	
Total Plant, Property and Equipment	**$47,000**	**$44,000**	**−6%**
Total Assets	**$94,400**	**$118,400**	**25%**
Liabilities and Owners' Equity			
Liabilities			
Current Liabilities			
Accounts Payable	$18,000	$21,600	**20%**
Total Current Liabilities	**$18,000**	**$21,600**	
Long-Term Liabilities			
Bank Loan Payable	$30,000	$30,000	
Total Long-Term Liabilities	**$30,000**	**$30,000**	
Total Liabilities	**$48,000**	**$51,600**	
Owners' Equity			
Owners' Investment	$30,000	$30,000	
Retained Earnings	$16,400	$36,800	**124%**
Total Owners' Equity	**$46,400**	**$66,800**	**44%**
Total Liabilities and Owners' Equity	**$94,400**	**$118,400**	**25%**

From the profit and loss statement, we see that Bonnie's Beachwear is now more profitable. The net profit of the business has grown 40 percent, from $5,471 in March to $7,681 in June.

The growth of profits over these three months has resulted in a 124-percent increase in retained earnings, from $16,400 to $36,800 ([36,800 - $16,400]/$16,400 = 124%). The growth in profits can also be seen in the cash balance of the business. Cash has grown 106 percent, from $20,400 to $42,000 over the three-month period.

Since revenue and cost of goods sold have increased, so has the store's inventory. In the asset section of the balance sheet, inventory has grown 20 percent, from $27,000 to $32,400, as the business continues to maintain 45 days sales in inventory. We also see that accounts payable have risen 20 percent to reflect the increased cost of inventory purchases.

While the increase in sales didn't affect the plant, property and equipment assets, we see that the value of plant, property and equipment has declined by 6 percent. This is a result of depreciating the computer equipment and furniture and fixtures owned by the business for an additional three months. An additional $3,000 of depreciation has been recognized, and the value of plant, property and equipment has fallen from $47,000 to $44,000.

Overall, total assets, total liabilities, and owners' equity have grown 25 percent, from $94,400 to $118,400.

As is the case with the profit and loss statement, we see varying growth rates for different items on the balance sheet.

Comparing Alternatives Using Growth Rates

One other use of growth rates is to compare the results of two different scenarios. Suppose that instead of doubling her advertising expense as a means of increasing sales, Bonnie instead decided to lower her price.

Take a look at the profit and loss statement for Bonnie's Beachwear in June 2010, assuming that Bonnie lowered her prices (see page 207). The average sale now generates $45 instead of $50, and sales volume increased from 1,000 units per month to 1,200 as a result of the lower prices, a 20-percent increase.

Bonnie's Beachwear Profit and Loss Statement (with Lower Prices)	March 2010	June 2010	Growth Rates
Sales Activities			
Revenue	$50,000	$54,000	*8%*
Cost of Goods Sold	$18,000	$21,600	*20%*
Gross Profit	**$32,000**	**$32,400**	*1%*
Operating Expenses			
Selling Expenses			
Advertising	$2,000	$2,000	*0%*
Sales Staff Salary	$10,000	$11,000	*10%*
General and Administrative			
Rent	$3,000	$3,000	
Utilities	$1,500	$1,500	
Owners' Salary	$4,500	$4,500	
Accounting, Payroll and Legal	$1,000	$1,000	
Depreciation	$833	$833	
Total Operating Expenses	$22,833	$23,833	*4%*
Operating Profit	**$9,167**	**$8,567**	*–7%*
Interest	$750	$750	
Profit Before Taxes	**$8,417**	**$7,817**	
Income Taxes @ 35%	$2,946	$2,736	
Net Profit	**$5,471**	**$5,081**	*–7%*

At the lower prices, a 200-unit increase in sales volume generates only $4,000 in additional revenue, an 8-percent increase. The average cost of the bathing suits and beachwear remains at $18, so a 200-unit (20 percent) increase in sales results in a 20-percent growth in cost of goods sold. Cost of goods sold has risen from $18,000 to $21,600. As cost of goods sold has grown at a greater rate than revenue, gross profit has only increased 1 percent, from $32,000 to $32,400. Reducing the sales price has increased volume by 20 percent, but has only generated 1-percent growth in gross profit.

As a result of the increase in sales volume, the sales staff salary expense has increased by 10 percent, from $10,000 to $11,000 per month. This is due to the extra sales staff time needed in the store to support the increased volume. This $1,000 boost in sales staff salary has led to a 4-percent increase in operating expenses.

As a result of the new pricing strategy, both the operating profit and net profit of the business have fallen by 7 percent. Translation: The business is 7-percent less profitable selling 1,200 units at $45 each than it is selling 1,000 units at $50 per unit.

One other use of GROWTH RATES is to compare the results of two different scenarios.

As we discussed in previous chapters, Bonnie's Beachwear uses a customer-centric operating strategy, focused on customer service, and hopes to earn high margins on its products. As this scenario shows, by reducing its prices, Bonnie's Beachwear has reduced its margins and yet it still has the higher operating expenses that result from its customer-centric strategy. The result of the lower prices, without a corresponding reduction in operating expenses, is a lower level of profits.

By using growth rates to analyze the changes in various items on the profit and loss statement and the balance sheet, Bonnie will be able to determine the effect each of the alternatives will have on the profitability of the business before a decision is made on which option to implement. Growth rates can help Bonnie make the most profitable decision.

If Bonnie had used growth rates to analyze her options, she would have chosen to keep the price at $50 per unit and grow sales through increased advertising.

CHAPTER FIFTEEN

Using Financial Tools to Manage Your Business

 The prior chapters have presented a series of tools that can be used to analyze financial statements and identify how your business stacks up against the competition and the industry. In this chapter, we bring together these lessons and summarize how these tools can be used to evaluate the effectiveness of your business strategies and the management of your cash during the operation and growth of your company.

Focus on Your Strategy

We began this book by discussing the need for any company to have a strategy that will allow the business to differentiate itself from the competition and build a competitive advantage. Creating and maintaining a competitive advantage is one of the keys to making money.

In Chapter 1, we introduced the four key strategies a business can use to create a competitive advantage:

1. Innovation and design
2. Operations
3. Sales and marketing
4. Customer service

We also discussed the need for a business to be either customer-centric or operational-centric. A customer-centric business competes by providing high value to its customers, while an operational-centric business competes by providing its products and services very efficiently.

Customer-Centric

A customer-centric business focuses on providing real or perceived value to customers so they are willing to pay more for the business's products or services.

A customer-centric business needs to be able to translate this CUSTOMER FOCUS into a higher price.

The key strategies for a customer-centric business are innovation and design, sales and marketing, or customer service. When used effectively, each of these strategies will help the business provide products or services that have value to the customer.

When a product or service has a real or perceived value to customers, they should be willing to pay a higher price for the product or service. Hence, a successful customer-centric business will be able to charge a higher price for its product or service.

A business that's using one of the customer-centric strategies and doesn't obtain a higher price for its products or services is either not effective in the use of the strategy, or hasn't correctly priced its products. A customer-centric business needs to be able to translate this customer focus into a higher price.

Businesses that are able to successfully implement customer-centric strategies include pharmaceutical companies; manufacturers of medical, scientific, and specialty equipment; name-brand consumer goods manufacturers; and some clothing and specialty retailers.

Businesses that use customer-centric strategies will have higher operating expenses. For example, a business that uses an innovation and design strategy typically will have to spend money to develop and design its products. This cost will be reflected in its operating expenses. Likewise, a business that uses a sales and marketing strategy will have higher operating expenses associated with its sales and marketing efforts, and a company that uses a customer service strategy will have higher operating expenses that reflect the costs of providing this customer service.

A business using a customer-centric strategy must be able to translate the higher price it receives for its products and services into a higher gross margin. This higher gross margin will allow it to pay the higher operating expenses and still earn a profit. If a customer-centric business isn't able to obtain sufficient prices or margins, it won't make money.

Operational-Centric

An operational-centric business is the opposite of a customer-centric business in many ways. Instead of focusing on differentiating their products to obtain a higher price, operational-centric businesses concentrate on manufacturing and distributing their products as efficiently as possible.

The gross margins for businesses pursuing an operational-centric strategy are low. Customers perceive very little difference between companies and are less willing to pay a higher price for products that they perceive to be very similar. As we noted in the examples in the earlier chapters of Part 3, this can include food and beverage retailers, oil and gas retailers, discount and low-price retailers, as well as manufacturers of many consumer goods.

As a result of earning lower gross margins, an operational-centric business must also have lower operating expenses because it won't be able to spend significant amounts of money on innovation and design, sales and marketing, or customer service. The operating expenses must remain low so the business can obtain sufficient operating profit and net profit.

Although its gross margins are low, an operational-centric business often has a large sales volume. This large sales volume allows the business to make a sufficient gross profit so it has money available to pay its operating and other expenses.

An operational-centric business that doesn't CONTROL its cost of goods sold and operating expenses won't make MONEY.

An operational-centric business that doesn't control its cost of goods sold and operating expenses won't make money. An operational-centric business with a low sales volume may also have difficulty making money.

In many instances, a customer-centric business develops into an operational-centric business as its products mature, become more accepted in the marketplace, and competitors begin offering the same products. When this switch occurs, a business that had been customer-centric will need to switch strategies to become more operational-centric and reduce its operating expenses accordingly.

This switch from customer-centric to operational-centric occurs frequently in the market. For example, a business that introduces a new electronic product is able for a time to earn high margins on that product. As other competitors develop similar products, the margins begin to fall, and successful businesses in the market must pursue an operations strategy rather than an innovation and design one. A similar event takes place in the clothing and fashion industry. For a time, a new product is able to earn high margins due to its desirability and uniqueness, but over time the product will become widely available, margins will fall, and to remain successful, a business manufacturing or selling these products will need to pursue an operational-centric strategy.

Focus on Your Cash

Many of the earlier chapters in this book have focused on cash. Chapters 3 and 4 focused on the contents and importance of the cash flow statement. Chapter 6 discussed the difference between cash and profit, and why a profitable business needs both. Chapter 11 focused on a business's working capital and ways to measure how efficiently a company is managing its cash. Chapters 12 and 13 focused on the ratios that can be used to tell if a business can pay its bills and pay the bank.

This leads us to a very important rule: To be profitable, a business must manage its cash. The most common reason a business will fail is that it runs out of cash. Without cash, a business won't be able to pay its bills, pay its staff, or pay its owners.

A business can run out of cash when:

- It's not converting its inventory into cash fast enough.
- It has too much cash tied up in inventory.
- It offers payment terms that are too generous.
- It's growing too fast and doesn't have enough cash available to support its growth.

For a business to be successful, it will need cash for operations and growth. The business owner must be aware of the amount of cash needed to keep the business operating and to grow the business.

Operating the Business

In Chapter 11, we introduced the concepts of working capital and efficiency ratios. Working capital is the difference between current assets and current liabilities, or the amount of cash that must be left in the business so bills can be paid as they come due.

Efficiency ratios measure how many days of inventory stays in the business before it's sold, how quickly the company collects payment from its customers, and how fast the business pays its suppliers. Collectively, efficiency ratios can be used to calculate a business's cash conversion cycle and measure how quickly it's able to convert its inventory into cash.

The more quickly a business is able to convert its inventory into cash, the less working capital it will need. A business can use several strategies to increase its cash conversion cycle.

One of the most effective strategies is to reduce the number of days in inventory. Purchasing inventory costs businesses money. To the extent that the amount of inventory a business carries can be reduced, the profitability of the business can be increased.

To be PROFITABLE, a business must MANAGE its cash.

This is the secret behind the just-in-time inventory system made popular by the Japanese automakers. Rather than purchasing a significant amount of raw materials and production parts ahead of time, automakers make purchases a day or two ahead of the production process, thereby minimizing the amount (and cost) of the inventory they purchase.

While it's more difficult for a retail business to use a just-in-time inventory process because the store needs merchandise on the shelves, it's often possible to receive more frequent deliveries from suppliers and reduce the amount (and cost) of inventory stored in the warehouse or in the back room.

Accountants classify inventory as an asset. From an operations perspective, inventory is an asset that has a cost to the business, and a company that minimizes the inventory it owns can increase its profitability.

A business can also increase its cash conversion cycle by managing and monitoring its collection and payment period.

As discussed in Chapter 11, retailers and consumer-focused services typically get paid very close to the time of sale, while manufacturers, business service organizations, and medical practices often get paid in 30 to 90 days or more.

It's often impossible for a small business that sells to a large customer to dictate its payment terms. The small business will have a collection period that reflects the terms offered by its large customers and the practices of the industry. In these instances, a business will need to make sure it has sufficient cash available to pay its bills as it waits for payment from its large customers.

As a business grows, the amount of WORKING CAPITAL needed grows as well.

A business will have much more success in setting its payment terms when dealing with businesses of comparable size. However, just because a business isn't able to establish its collection period in all instances doesn't mean it shouldn't monitor its collection period. The business owner or manager should be aware of the payment terms extended to customers and monitor the collection period for adherence to these terms. In this way, the business can be assured it's collecting its cash as efficiently as possible. Likewise, the owner or manager should be aware of payment terms offered by its suppliers and should take as long to pay its bills as its suppliers allow.

Growing the Business

As a business grows, the amount of working capital needed grows as well. That's why the cash conversion cycle of a business is so critically important. The faster a business is able to receive cash for the sale of products, the less working capital it will need. If a business has a long cash conversion cycle, it will need more working capital to grow than if it has a short cash conversion cycle.

When a business grows and needs more cash for working capital, there are three possible sources of this cash:

1. Additional investment by the business owner
2. Borrowing from the bank or another lender
3. Cash generated from operations

A business that wants to grow quickly will generally need a significant additional owners' investment or will need to borrow. If a business borrows, it will incur additional interest expenses associated with these borrowings.

However, if a business chooses to grow more slowly, it may be able to generate the additional cash it needs from its operating activities and the efficient management of its cash conversion cycle. A company that chooses this path won't incur extra interest expenses and won't require additional investment from the owner.

As the company grows, it's critical that the business owner or manager understands the cash needs of the business as more units are sold or more services are provided. It's also important that they've identified a source of this cash to fund this growth. If the business grows too rapidly and doesn't have the cash available to fund this growth, the business could very easily run out of cash and find itself unable to pay its bills.

Use Your Tools

To summarize, let's review the ways financial tools can help you create and keep a profitable business.

- Profitable businesses will use customer-centric or operational-centric strategies to obtain a competitive advantage.

- Profitable businesses will translate a high gross margin into a higher operating profit and net profit.

- The faster businesses are able to turn over inventory, the more profitable they will be.

- Businesses can achieve cost savings by minimizing the amount of inventory.

- Companies can become more profitable by improving their cash collection cycle.

- Businesses should only grow to the extent they can obtain the working capital (cash) to support their growth.

Financial tools can also be used to identify situations where the profitability of the business may decline:

- If the business has a high gross margin but also has high operating expenses, this high gross margin may not translate to a higher operating profit or higher net profit.
- If margins fall, the business may be less profitable.
- If the inventory turnover of a business slows, the company may be less profitable.
- If the cash collection cycle increases, the business will need more cash and may be less profitable.
- If growth reduces margins, significantly increases interest expenses, or requires too much working capital, growing the business will not be a profitable strategy.
- If a business doesn't use a customer-centric or operational-centric strategy, then it's hard to create a profitable business.

Now that we've looked at the tools that can be used to evaluate the operations of a business, we'll examine how these tools can be used to start and grow a business. This is the subject of the next part of the book.

Part Four

Building and Operating Your Business to Make Money

In earlier chapters of this book, we discussed the common financial statements that businesses use and introduced a series of tools that business owners or managers can use to analyze their financial statements and understand how their business makes money. We also discussed why it's important that a business use a strategy to gain a competitive advantage in the marketplace.

In Part 4, we'll discuss how to forecast the startup and operations of a business and how these financial analysis tools can be used to help the owner create a profitable business. We'll also review the importance of taxes and accounting to the business owner and help you prepare to meet with lenders and investors.

CHAPTER SIXTEEN

What to Consider When Starting Your Business

 To many people, the thought of starting and operating a business is a daunting task. While operating a business can have many benefits, it's also hard work.

- Entrepreneurs typically work much more than a 40-hour work week.

- Entrepreneurship requires self-discipline and a commitment to build a business.

- Entrepreneurship often requires a substantial commitment of money by the founders of the business.

- Entrepreneurship requires that an individual become involved in all aspects of the business, from making photocopies to meeting with bankers and major customers.

- Finally, entrepreneurship requires a commitment on the part of the entrepreneur's family. To succeed, an entrepreneur will need support and guidance from those closest to him or her.

If you've read this far, you've probably already gone through the personal introspection necessary to start a successful business. You comprehend the commitment necessary to start and grow a successful business, and you know that understanding finance is critical to making money from a business.

In the remainder of this chapter we'll discuss what you should consider when starting your business.

Use Your Expertise

The first element to consider is what products or services you'll offer. This seems like an easy decision, but choosing the right product or services helps define the structure and strategy of the business.

From the discussion in previous chapters, it should be apparent that there are many different types of products and services a business can offer. It should also be evident that the profits available to a business owner can differ depending on the products and services offered.

You should choose something you're PASSIONATE about.

Ideally, one of the first tasks you should undertake when you consider starting a business is an evaluation of your strengths and weaknesses, and an assessment of what you want to spend your day doing.

If you're going to form a business and spend a significant part of your time working to build this business, you should choose something you're passionate about. If you're not passionate, you may find it difficult to remain dedicated to building the business. You may find your business to be just another job, and you may find that as a job, it's less rewarding than the one you just left. To be successful, you *must* be passionate.

Next, you should understand your strengths and weaknesses. In the last chapter, we discussed the need for businesses to pursue either a customer-centric or operational-centric strategy. We also indicated that it's very difficult for a business to have both an operational-centric and customer-centric focus simultaneously. A business can be strong in only one of these areas.

It's the same when analyzing your strengths and weaknesses. Your strength may be in sales and marketing, managing or operating the business, designing products, or in working to serve the needs of customers. Chances are, you won't be good at all these things, and, in fact, you might not even have a desire to perform some of these tasks.

We can't stress enough the IMPORTANCE of RESEARCHING typical margins for your product or service.

As a business owner you should recognize that you can't be good at everything and that you should focus your time and energy on the things that you are good at, and hire staff or partner with others in those areas in which your skills are weaker.

For instance, in our Uptown Chiropractic example, Dr. Press planned to spend a significant portion of his time on his strength—providing services to customers (i.e., treating patients). He intended to spend a smaller amount of his time on his weakness—administering the business—so he planned to hire staff to deal with bookkeeping and submitting claims to insurance companies.

Likewise, in our example of Bonnie's Beachwear, Bonnie planned to use the skills she learned working as an executive in the retail fashion industry to create a business that catered to a fashion-conscious, high-end clientele. She planned to hire sales staff to work the floor in the store and wait on the customers.

Finally, as Boutique Handbags expanded and moved its operations from Ann Marie's house to a manufacturing facility, Ann Marie chose to continue designing and marketing the handbags (her strengths) and planned to hire staff to work in the manufacturing process.

A business owner might also recognize that the roles the owner must play will change over time as the business grows. When a business is young, the owner may have to step in and fill many roles. As the business grows, the owner will be able to hire staff to focus on the areas where he/she is weakest, and spend his/her time focused on the areas where he/she is strongest.

Your strengths will also help you define what strategy you should use to operate the business and to define how you'll achieve a competitive advantage.

Again looking at our example of Bonnie's Beachwear, we see that Bonnie developed an expertise in the clothing business while working for corporations in the fashion industry. From her time with these corporations, Bonnie understands how the high-end fashion industry works and how retail stores catering to high-end customers operate. These are her strengths, and she used these strengths in opening Bonnie's Beachwear.

Given these strengths, Bonnie would have been much less likely to open a discount clothing store or to switch industries and open a food store. Neither of these businesses would have capitalized on her strengths.

Alternatively, Bonnie could have chosen to create a service business providing consulting services to the fashion industry or specialty clothing stores, or perhaps started a business manufacturing or importing fashion products. Each of these might have used her strengths as well.

When starting out, you should select a product or service where your strengths will allow you to identify and implement a strategy that you can use to create a competitive advantage for your business.

Margins

It's very important in the planning stage that you research the typical margins for your products and services and define the margins you expect to earn from your business.

As you'll recall from the last chapter, a business that uses a customer-centric strategy will need to earn high gross margins to support the additional operating expenses associated with serving its customers. If you're planning to use a customer-centric strategy, and won't earn high gross margins, you should reconsider your business strategy as you most likely won't be profitable after paying the higher operating expenses.

Likewise, if you're planning to use an operational-centric strategy but don't expect to generate a sufficient sales volume, you may find that your business is unable to cover operating expenses or earn a profit.

Minimizing the amount of WORKING CAPITAL used in the business helps increase PROFITABILITY.

In Chapter 10, we discussed typical margins—gross margins, operating margins, and net margins—for many different types of businesses. We also talked about where you might look for sources of margin information such as the U.S. Census Bureau website or our website at www.FinanceWithoutFear.com.

We can't stress enough the importance of researching typical margins for your product or service. You'll need to understand how much you can expect to earn on each sale, the operating expenses that are standard for your industry, and how much profit you can anticipate the business to earn. This information is necessary in order to develop financial projections for your business.

As you develop your financial projections, it's also important to determine how your margins are the same or different from others in the industry. If your margins are significantly different, you should be able to explain why. If your margins are worse than those typical for the industry, you may be projecting a business that's not as profitable as its competitors. You also may be projecting a business that doesn't have a competitive advantage, and, in fact, doesn't make money.

If, on the other hand, your margins are better than those typical for the industry, you'll need an explanation for this as well. Your investors and bankers will want to know how you expect to earn higher margins than the industry norm. You should be able to answer this question for yourself as well—before you invest in your business.

In general, the answer to this question will come from your strategy and competitive advantage. You should be able to point to one or more elements in the operation of your business that will provide you with a competitive advantage. Your product may be patented or in some other way be difficult for your competitors to imitate. Your business may be located in a particularly attractive location where you expect to be able to draw a higher volume of customers, or you may be an expert in a consulting niche that allows you to charge a premium price for your services. Whatever the reason, you must be able to identify and articulate it if you expect your business to earn margins that are significantly different than the industry.

Products

As you plan your business, it's important that you focus on the goods and services you'll sell. In your planning, you should research:

- The type of products you plan to sell
- The type of services you plan to offer
- The prices your competitors charge for these products and services

You might also consider whether your competitors are using customer-centric or operational-centric strategies.

You should also identify:

- The potential suppliers of your raw materials and inventory
- Any differences in the type, quality or features of the raw materials and inventory available that might affect the value your customers get from your products

- How much it will cost to purchase these raw materials or inventory
- The terms under which suppliers will sell to your business

The last point is very important. As we discussed previously, the amount of working capital required by a business is dependent on its cash conversion cycle and a key element of the cash conversion cycle is the payment period, that is, the amount of time the company has to pay its suppliers.

If different suppliers are offering raw materials or inventory of comparable quality but with different payment terms, your business will use less cash and be more profitable if you purchase from the supplier that offers the most generous payment terms.

It's very important that you develop REALISTIC PROJECTIONS of how much cash you'll need to get started and operate.

You should also identify the prospective purchasers of your products or services and research the payment terms these customers require. As we discussed previously, if you're selling to large customers or being reimbursed for your services by a third party such as the government or insurance companies, you will most likely have your collection period dictated by these customers.

However, if customers require different payment periods or you're able to dictate the payment period, selling to customers with the most favorable payment terms will provide your business with the shortest collection period. The shorter the collection period, the less cash will be required by your business.

You should also research how quickly others in the industry turn over their inventory and determine whether you anticipate turning over your inventory at a rate that's similar, faster or slower. If your inventory turnover rate is quicker, your business will have a faster collection cycle and may require less working capital. If your inventory turnover rate is slower, you'll have a slower collection cycle and may require more working capital. Minimizing the amount of working capital used in the business helps increase profitability.

Cash

The startup of any business requires cash. Often, the startup of a business requires a significant amount of cash. One of the keys to starting a business is to identify your cash needs and to identify potential sources of that cash.

The next chapter focuses on how to project initial cash flows and cash needs for your business. Later chapters in Part 4 discuss how to project and analyze the cash needs of a growing business. Additionally, the *Finance Without Fear Business Forecasting Workbook* provides a step-by-step process for forecasting the operations and cash needs of your business.

When starting a business, it's very important that you develop realistic projections of how much cash you'll need to get started and to operate. Once you have these projections, you can determine if you have sufficient cash available to begin the business or if you need to identify other sources of cash.

The initial cash investment in any business comes from the owner. Typically, the first investment in a business is made from the owner's savings. If the startup needs additional money, the owner will often get a home equity loan or will borrow on his or her credit cards.

After the owner has invested his/her cash, friends and family often provide investments in the form of loans or additional equity.

Once a business is up and running, banks and other lenders are more likely to provide loans. It's very difficult for a startup to obtain funding from a bank. However, sometimes businesses that aren't yet bankable are able to obtain financing from community loan funds.

By identifying your cash needs and sources of cash as you start up, your business will be less likely to run out of cash as it begins operations and you'll be more likely to have created a profitable business.

Return

The final thing you should consider when starting your business is the return the business will generate.

We began this chapter by pointing out that starting a new business should be a labor of love. An entrepreneur should expect to spend many hours per week working in his/her new business.

If you plan to dedicate a significant number of your waking hours each week to this business, there should be a financial return. If your business isn't going to make money and provide you with a sufficient financial return, you should question whether it's a viable investment and how long you'll be interested in spending your time on it.

The returns should be SUFFICIENT to COMPENSATE the owners and investors for the time spent starting the BUSINESS.

In Chapter 10, we introduced the concepts of return on assets and return on equity. These ratios measure the returns the business will pay its owners. The returns should be sufficient to compensate the owners and investors for the time spent starting the business and for the risk they've taken with their money by investing it in the business.

As you project the cash flows and ongoing operations of your business, you must keep in mind the financial return you'll receive. It's not uncommon to develop financial projections only to realize that the business won't provide a sufficient return to justify the owners' investment. If the projections indicate the business won't make money or generate sufficient returns, it's probably best if you don't continue to pursue its creation.

However, if the projections indicate that the business will make money and generate sufficient returns, this indicates that you've created a business that will justify the time and money required to build it.

CHAPTER SEVENTEEN

Starting Your Business

There's an old saying that "you have to spend money to make money." Anyone who has ever started a business certainly knows this to be true. In order to start a business, the owner must spend money to set up operations and will need to have enough money to pay expenses while waiting for payment from sales to begin.

In this chapter, we'll once again use Bonnie's Beachwear as our sample business. The startup of Bonnie's Beachwear is typical of many businesses:

- First, it must find and rent a location for the store.
- Next, the business must spend some money to renovate and outfit the store.
- The owner will need to begin working full time to get the business up and running.
- The business will need to purchase some inventory to stock the store ahead of the grand opening.
- Sales staff will need to be hired.
- Money will need to be spent on advertising and marketing.

- The business will have a grand opening and begin to generate cash that can be used to pay its bills.

Setting Up the Business

It may take several months before a business is able to open its doors and several more months before the sales volume grows to a sufficient level to cover operating expenses.

For an establishment like Bonnie's Beachwear, it might take two months from the time the lease is signed until Bonnie's is able to open its doors to customers. During this time, Bonnie's would renovate and outfit its store, begin advertising its business, hire the sales staff, and purchase its initial supply of inventory from its suppliers.

In Chapter 2, we discussed Bonnie's startup expenses. It was expected to cost the business $40,000 to renovate its store and install carpeting and upscale fitting rooms, purchase higher-end merchandise display racks, and buy wooden furniture and customer service desks. Additionally, the business was planning on spending $10,000 to purchase computerized cash registers, a computer for the office, and inventory management software. Overall, the one-time startup expenses for furniture, fixtures and equipment would be $50,000. During these two months, the business will also need to pay $10,000 per month in general and administrative expenses: $3,000 for rent, $1,500 for utilities, $1,000 for legal services to incorporate the business, and $4,500 in salary to the owner who will be working full time to set up the business.

Finally, prior to the grand opening, Bonnie's Beachwear will also want to begin advertising the business, make its initial inventory purchases, and hire and train the sales staff.

Bonnie plans to begin advertising immediately at a cost of $2,000 per month. She also plans to have the new sales staff begin working two weeks before the grand opening. During this time, the staff can be trained and can stock the inventory on the display racks in the store. For these two weeks, the sales staff will cost the business $5,000.

Bonnie also plans to make an initial inventory purchase of 500 bathing suits and beachwear apparel items during the second month. This inventory will cost the business $9,000. However, the suppliers will allow the business 30 days to pay, so this purchase won't have to be paid for until the third month.

In total, in addition to the $50,000 of one-time startup expenses, the business will incur $12,000 in operating expenses during the first month, and $17,000 in operating expenses during the second (including the cost of the sales staff), before it has even opened its doors to the public.

In our example, Bonnie's Beachwear will have incurred expenses totaling $79,000 before it even opens its doors. The projected cash payments during the first two months of operations for Bonnie's Beachwear are shown in the chart below.

Bonnie's Beachwear
Projected Cash Flow
First 2 Months of Operations

	Month 1	Month 2
Cash Paid		
Startup Expenses		
Furniture and Fixtures	$40,000	
Computer Equipment	$10,000	
Inventory Costs		
Payments to Suppliers	$0	$0
Selling Expenses		
Sales Staff	$0	$5,000
Advertising	$2,000	$2,000
General and Administrative		
Rent	$3,000	$3,000
Utilities	$1,500	$1,500
Owners' Salary	$4,500	$4,500
Accounting, Payroll and Legal	$1,000	$1,000
Interest Paid	$0	$0
Income Taxes Paid	$0	$0
Total Cash Paid	**$62,000**	**$17,000**

Building Sales Volume

Now let's look at Bonnie's operations during months three and four. During this period, Bonnie's has opened its doors and is selling beachwear to its customers, but it doesn't yet have sufficient volume to generate positive cash flow.

Let's start by checking the inventory and sales volume of Bonnie's Beachwear during these two months. The "Inventory and Sales Volume" chart on page 235 shows the inventory that Bonnie's is receiving from its suppliers as well as the number of units of beachwear it's selling to customers. As you can see, as it builds sales volume, Bonnie's Beachwear is purchasing more inventory than it's selling. Bonnie's needs to purchase the inventory ahead of sales in order to have inventory in the store for customers to purchase.

It's very RARE when a business is able to open its doors and ACHIEVE a high sales VOLUME immediately.

During month two, Bonnie's purchased 500 units of bathing suits and beachwear apparel and sold none.

During month three, Bonnie's purchased an additional 500 units of bathing suits and beachwear, and sold 250 units it purchased in month two. At the end of month three, Bonnie's had 750 units of inventory on hand.

During month four, in anticipation of a growing sales volume, Bonnie's purchased 750 units of bathing suits and beachwear apparel and sold 500, leaving the business with 1,000 bathing suits and beachwear items in inventory.

Bonnie's Beachwear
Inventory and Sales Volume
First 4 Months of Operations

Inventory and Sales Volume	Month 1	Month 2	Month 3	Month 4
Inventory Purchased from Suppliers	0	500	500	750
Units Sold to Customers	0	0	250	500
Units of Inventory on Hand	**0**	**500**	**750**	**1,000**
Inventory Payment to Suppliers	0	0	500	500
Payment Received for Units Sold	0	0	250	500

Now let's investigate how the sales volume and level of inventory purchases affects the cash flow of the business. The projected cash flow for Bonnie's Beachwear for months three and four is shown in the chart below.

Bonnie's Beachwear Projected Cash Flow
Months 3 and 4 of Operations

	Month 3	Month 4
Cash Received		
Revenue	$12,500	$25,000
Total Cash Received	**$12,500**	**$25,000**
Cash Paid		
Startup Expenses		
Furniture and Fixtures		
Computer Equipment		
Inventory Costs		
Payments to Suppliers	$9,000	$9,000
Selling Expenses		
Sales Staff	$10,000	$10,000
Advertising	$2,000	$2,000
General and Administrative		
Rent	$3,000	$3,000
Utilities	$1,500	$1,500
Owners' Salary	$4,500	$4,500
Accounting, Payroll and Legal	$1,000	$1,000
Total Cash Paid	**$31,000**	**$31,000**
Net Cash Flow	**($18,500)**	**($6,000)**

The projected cash flow statement for months three and four shows several things. First, we see that the business has opened its doors and has begun to earn revenue from the sale of bathing suits and other beach apparel. The business earned $12,500 of revenue in the third month when it sold 250 items and $25,000 of revenue in the fourth month when it sold 500 items.

However, if we look at the last line on this statement, we see that the business has a negative cash flow for each of these months. In both of these months, the business is spending more cash than it's receiving from sales. The business must pay its suppliers $9,000 each month for the inventory it purchased in the prior month and must pay $22,000 each month for selling and general and administrative expenses.

Bonnie's Beachwear is paying out $31,000 in cash in months three and four, yet it's only receiving $12,500 in cash in month three and $25,000 in cash in month four.

The business isn't yet selling enough beachwear each month to generate the cash to cover its operating expenses and pay its suppliers. In total, the business pays out $24,500 more cash than it receives in these two months. In months one and two, before Bonnie's Beachwear opened its doors, the business used $79,000 in cash, and during the third and fourth months, the business used $24,500 more cash than it received.

In order for Bonnie's to survive its first four months in business, it will need to have $103,500 in cash.

Positive Cash Flow

Finally, let's look at Bonnie's operations during months five and six. During these two months, the sales volume of the business continues to grow. The business sells 750 units of bathing suits and beachwear apparel in month five and 1,000 units in month six. The business has also increased its inventory purchases to

1,000 units per month to make sure it has sufficient inventory on hand to meet customer demand.

The chart below shows the inventory and sales volume for the first six months of operations.

Bonnie's Beachwear
Inventory and Sales Volume
First 6 Months of Operations

	Month 1	Month 2	Month 3	Month 4	Month 5	Month 6
Inventory and Sales Volume						
Inventory Purchased from Suppliers	0	500	500	750	1,000	1,000
Units Sold to Customers	0	0	250	500	750	1,000
Units of Inventory on Hand	**0**	**500**	**750**	**1,000**	**1,250**	**1,250**
Inventory Payment to Suppliers	0	0	500	500	750	1,000
Payment Received for Units Sold	0	0	250	500	750	1,000

Now let's look at how this increased volume affects the cash flow of Bonnie's Beachwear. The projected cash flow for Bonnie's Beachwear in months five and six is shown in the chart on page 238.

Bonnie's Beachwear Projected Cash Flow
Months 5 and 6 of Operations

	Month 5	Month 6
Cash Received		
Revenue	$37,500	$50,000
Total Cash Received	$37,500	$50,000
Cash Paid		
Startup Expenses		
Furniture and Fixtures		
Computer Equipment		
Inventory Costs		
Payments to Suppliers	$13,500	$18,000
Selling Expenses		
Sales Staff	$10,000	$10,000
Advertising	$2,000	$2,000
General and Administrative		
Rent	$3,000	$3,000
Utilities	$1,500	$1,500
Owners' Salary	$4,500	$4,500
Accounting, Payroll and Legal	$1,000	$1,000
Total Cash Paid	$35,500	$40,000
Net Cash Flow	$2,000	$10,000

As the sales volume increases, so does the revenue of the business. The business receives $37,500 by selling 750 units in month five and $50,000 by selling 1,000 units in month six.

After deducting payments to suppliers and operating expenses, Bonnie's has a projected positive cash flow of $2,000 in month five and a projected positive cash flow of $10,000 in month six.

Based on our projections, if Bonnie's Beachwear is able to sell more than 750 units per month, the business will have a positive cash flow. If Bonnie's is able to survive to month five, the business will be generating more cash than it's using and will be able to pay its bills. All that's necessary is $103,500 in cash that will allow the business to survive its first four months of operation.

Seeking Startup Capital

Where is Bonnie's Beachwear going to get this cash that will allow it to survive for the first four months? As discussed in Chapter 16, the primary source of capital for any new business is an investment by the owner, who typically invests money from his/her savings and may also borrow funds, using home equity loans or cash advances on credit cards. Beyond the owners' initial investment, friends and family also often are called upon to invest in the business. A business might also borrow a portion of the startup and working capital it needs from a lender such as a bank or a community loan fund.

In our example of Bonnie's Beachwear, let's assume that Bonnie personally invests $45,000 in the business, and the business obtains a $65,000 loan from a local bank at a 12% interest rate. This will provide the business with $110,000 in cash to start up the business and allow it to operate for the first four months. The complete cash flow projection for the first six months of operations of Bonnie's Beachwear is shown in the chart on page 240.

Bonnie's Beachwear
Projected Cash Flow
First 6 Months of Operations

	Month 1	Month 2	Month 3	Month 4	Month 5	Month 6
Cash Received						
Owners' Investment	$45,000					
Bank Financing	$65,000					
Revenue	$0	$0	$12,500	$25,000	$37,500	$50,000
Total Cash Received	**$110,000**	**$0**	**$12,500**	**$25,000**	**$37,500**	**$50,000**
Cash Paid						
Startup Expenses						
Furniture and Fixtures	$40,000					
Computer Equipment	$10,000					
Inventory Costs						
Payments to Suppliers	$0	$0	$9,000	$9,000	$13,500	$18,000
Selling Expenses						
Sales Staff	$0	$5,000	$10,000	$10,000	$10,000	$10,000
Advertising	$2,000	$2,000	$2,000	$2,000	$2,000	$2,000
General and Administrative						
Rent	$3,000	$3,000	$3,000	$3,000	$3,000	$3,000
Utilities	$1,500	$1,500	$1,500	$1,500	$1,500	$1,500
Owners' Salary	$4,500	$4,500	$4,500	$4,500	$4,500	$4,500
Accounting, Payroll and Legal	$1,000	$1,000	$1,000	$1,000	$1,000	$1,000
Interest Paid	$650	$650	$650	$650	$650	$650
Income Taxes Paid	$0	$0	$0	$0	$181	$2,981
Total Cash Paid	**$62,650**	**$17,650**	**$31,650**	**$31,650**	**$36,331**	**$43,631**
Net Cash Flow	**$47,350**	**($17,650)**	**($19,150)**	**($6,650)**	**$1,169**	**$6,369**
Beginning of Period Cash	$0	$47,350	$29,700	$10,550	$3,900	$5,069
Plus Net Cash Flow	$47,350	($17,650)	($19,150)	($6,650)	$1,169	$6,369
End of Period Cash	**$47,350**	**$29,700**	**$10,550**	**$3,900**	**$5,069**	**$11,438**

This startup investment of $110,000 provides Bonnie's Beachwear with enough cash to launch the business and pay suppliers and operating expenses for the first four months, until the revenue from sales exceeds the monthly cash outflows. In other words, this $110,000 allows the business to survive until it becomes profitable.

How Much Money Does a Business Need?

One of your reactions as you read this chapter might be: "Wow, I need $110,000 to open a retail store. That can't be right. How much do I really need?"

The answer is very simple: A business needs enough money to pay its bills until its cash inflows exceed its cash outflows. Any business will need to pay some startup expenses and will need some cash to pay its bills until it begins to receive sufficient revenue. Depending on the circumstances and the type of business, it could be more than $110,000 or it could be less.

Startup Expenses

If you're beginning a business in your home, your startup expenses will generally be low. You might clean out your spare bedroom and purchase a desk, computer, printer and some business cards. You might even have a second telephone installed. With a quick visit to the local office supply store, you could probably equip your business for under $2,000.

However, if you're planning on locating your business in some place other than your spare bedroom, you'll certainly incur some startup expenses.

If you plan to manufacture products, you should expect some startup expenses to purchase the machinery and equipment needed for your manufacturing process. You may be able to minimize your expenses by leasing key pieces of equipment, but you'll most likely still have some startup expenses even if you plan on leasing. You may also be able to minimize your expenses by purchasing used rather than new equipment.

If you plan to open a retail store, you'll need to purchase inventory to stock the shelves, so there's merchandise available for customers to purchase. In most instances, you'll also need to spend some money improving the appearance of the store. This might include a new sign, a fresh coat of paint, some new carpeting, and new display racks. If you have a low-margin or operational-centric retail store, these expenses might be minimized. However, if your customer expects a high level of service and quality, you'll need to spend the extra money to outfit your store to meet these customer expectations.

Even professional service businesses should expect some startup expenses, which could range from a few thousand dollars to equip a simple legal or consulting office to several hundred thousand dollars to fully outfit a medical office.

In our Bonnie's Beachwear example, we assumed that the business catered to a high-end customer and had to pay $40,000 to renovate an entire store for that clientele. If Bonnie's was catering to a lower-end customer or had been able to find a store where some of the finish work had already been done, the business might not have needed to spend as much on outfitting the store.

Initial Operations

In addition to startup expenses, most ventures will need some cash that will allow them to pay the bills until the business is earning sufficient revenue. This could take one month, six months, or a year.

In the case of Bonnie's Beachwear, the business incurred expenses for two months while the owner prepared to open the doors to customers, and then spent two months where its sales revenue was too low to cover its operating expenses.

These two events are very typical for a startup business that's leasing a commercial location. There will always be a lag between when a business leases its space and when it's able to open for business. This lag may only be a few weeks if the rented space is in move-in condition, or it could be several months if substantial work is needed to get the space ready. During this time, the business incurs expenses for the rent and utilities and will also have expenses associated with preparing and moving into the space.

It's very rare when a business is able to open its doors and achieve a high sales volume immediately. In most cases, sales during the first few months will be slow, and the business will need to have cash available to pay its bills until it begins to earn sufficient revenue. In our example of Bonnie's Beachwear, we assumed this took two months. In many other cases, it might take longer. It's critical that a business plan for a low initial sales volume and set aside some startup capital to pay the bills during this period.

So back to the question that opened this section—how much startup money does a business need? To answer this question, the business owner or manager must develop a detailed estimate of startup expenses and a detailed estimate of the costs of operating the business until enough money is coming in from sales to pay the bills. Developing these estimates is a critical step in structuring a business to make money.

The *Finance Without Fear Business Forecasting Workbook* is a great resource to assist you in developing these estimates. The workbook will walk you through the steps of developing cash flow projections and startup expense estimates for your business.

CHAPTER EIGHTEEN

Planning and Budgeting Growth

In this chapter, we'll look at the process of growing a business. As you plan your business, you may be hoping to start out small and grow over time, or you may want to try developing a volume business immediately. In either case, in order to grow a business, you'll need cash. To know how much cash, you'll need to analyze your financial statements to determine how the growth will affect the financial position of the business and to figure out how much cash the business will need.

In this chapter, we'll use our professional service business, Uptown Chiropractic, as our example company, and examine how growth affects the profitability and cash needs of the business.

First-Year Operations

Uptown Chiropractic is a small chiropractic office owned by Dr. Eric Press that offers a full range of chiropractic treatments for back and neck stiffness, leg and arm pain, slipped disks, headaches, whiplash and sports injuries. The office includes three treatment rooms, an exam room, a patient waiting area, and a small office for Dr. Press. In addition to Dr. Press, the business employs two chiropractic assistants and part-time billing and bookkeeping staff. The key assumptions for the business include:

- With the current staff, the business is able to treat 400 patients per month.
- The major costs of the business are the salaries of Dr. Press at $5,000 per month and the two chiropractic assistants at a total cost of $4,500 per month.
- The business rents its office space at a cost of $2,000 per month. Utilities cost $1,000 per month.
- The business leases its treatment equipment at a cost of $4,500 per month.
- The business receives average revenue of $60 per patient treatment. Seventy-five percent of the patient treatments are reimbursed by insurance companies at $55 per treatment and 25 percent are paid directly by patients at $75 per treatment.
- It takes the insurance companies 120 days to reimburse Uptown Chiropractic for the treatments it has provided.
- Uptown Chiropractic must pay its monthly operating expenses and staff salaries while waiting for reimbursement from the insurance companies.
- The initial funding for the business came in the form of a $20,000 investment by Dr. Press and a $36,000 bank loan.

The chart on page 247 presents the profit and loss statement for Uptown Chiropractic for the year ending December 31, 2009, which is the end of the business's first year of operation. The business had revenue of $288,000 and earned a net profit of $15,730.

Uptown Chiropractic
First Year Profit and Loss Statement

Year Ending
Dec. 31, 2009

Sales Activities	
Revenue	$288,000
Cost of Services	
Doctor's Salary	$60,000
Assistants' Salaries	$54,000
Treatment Supplies	$24,000
Total Cost of Services	$138,000
Gross Profit	**$150,000**
Operating Expenses	
General and Administrative	
Rent	$24,000
Utilities	$12,000
Equipment Lease	$54,000
Bookkeeper/Billing Clerk	$18,000
Licenses, Certifications, Training	$6,000
Accounting, Payroll and Legal	$6,000
Total General and Administrative	$120,000
Depreciation	$1,000
Total Operating Expenses	$121,000
Operating Profit	**$29,000**
Interest	$4,800
Profit before Taxes	**$24,200**
Income Taxes @ 35%	$8,470
Net Profit	**$15,730**

The first year cash flow for Uptown Chiropractic is shown in the chart on page 249. The business has a positive cash flow for the year. However, this positive cash flow results from financing and investment activities and not from the operation of the business.

The business spent $281,270 in cash during the year while only receiving $238,500 in cash from operations. The cash flow is positive because of the owner's $20,000 investment and the receipt of a $36,000 bank loan.

Several startup events also adversely affected the cash flow of Uptown Chiropractic during its first year of operations. The business had a one-time expense of $10,000 to purchase furniture and computer equipment, and it didn't receive any reimbursement from the insurance companies until after the fourth month.

In the second year of operations, when Uptown Chiropractic is receiving reimbursement from the insurance companies for the full 12 months and it's not paying any startup expenses, the business can be expected to generate a positive cash flow of $16,730 from operations.

Uptown Chiropractic
First-Year Cash Flow Statement

Year Ending
Dec. 31, 2009

Cash Received	
Cash from Financing Activities	
Owners' Investment	$20,000
Bank Financing	$36,000
Total Cash from Financing Activities	**$56,000**
Cash from Operating Activities	
Revenue	
Cash Payments	$90,000
Insurance Reimbursement	$148,500
Total Cash from Operating Activities	**$238,500**
Total Cash Received	**$294,500**
Cash Paid	
Cash Used for Asset Activities	
Startup Expenses	
Furniture and Fixtures	$5,000
Computer Equipment	$5,000
Total Cash Used for Asset Activities	**$10,000**
Cash Used in Operating Activities	
Cost of Services	
Doctor's Salary	$60,000
Sr. Chiropractic Assistant	$30,000
Jr. Chiropractic Assistant	$24,000
Treatment Supplies	$24,000
General and Administrative	
Rent	$24,000
Utilities	$12,000
Equipment Lease	$54,000
Bookkeeper/Billing Clerk	$18,000
Licenses, Certifications, Training	$6,000
Accounting, Payroll and Legal	$6,000
Interest Paid	$4,800
Income Taxes Paid	$8,470
Total Cash Used in Operating Activities	**$271,270**
Total Cash Paid	**$281,270**
Net Cash Flow	**$13,230**
Beginning of Period Cash	**$0**
Plus Net Cash Flow	$13,230
End of Period Cash	**$13,230**

The balance sheet for Uptown Chiropractic after the first year of operations is presented below.

Uptown Chiropractic First-Year Balance Sheet	Year Ending Dec. 31, 2009
Assets	
Current Assets	
Cash	$13,230
Accounts Receivable	$49,500
Inventory	$0
Total Current Assets	**$62,730**
Plant, Property and Equipment	
Equipment	$10,000
Less: Accumulated Depreciation	($1,000)
Total Plant, Property and Equipment	**$9,000**
Total Assets	**$71,730**
Liabilities and Owners' Equity	
Liabilities	
Current Liabilities	
Accounts Payable	$0
Total Current Liabilities	**$0**
Long-Term Liabilities	
Loan from Bank	$36,000
Total Long-Term Liabilities	**$36,000**
Total Liabilities	**$36,000**
Owners' Equity	
Owners' Investment	$20,000
Retained Earnings	$15,730
Total Owners' Equity	**$35,730**
Total Liabilities and Owners' Equity	**$71,730**

As a professional services organization, its balance sheet is very simple. The only liability is the bank loan. Assets include a small cash position; accounts receivable, reflecting payments due from the insurance company; and the value of the office furniture and computers.

The most significant item is the $49,500 in accounts receivable due for patient treatments from the insurance companies, which represents the working capital position of the business. In order to treat 400 patients per month, Uptown Chiropractic needs $49,500 of working capital. In our example, this working capital was obtained from a bank loan and from the owner's personal investment.

Growing Uptown Chiropractic

After reviewing the first year of operations, Dr. Press looked at his profit and loss statement and realized that the business only made $15,730. He was hoping to have made more. It seemed that the larger chiropractic firm he left when he started his own business was very profitable.

Dr. Press decided to look at the financial effects of growing Uptown Chiropractic. He felt that if he hired a second doctor and another junior chiropractic assistant, he could increase the number of patient treatments from 400 to 800 per month.

Increasing the patient volume would require an office expansion. The current setup of three treatment rooms and one exam room was adequate for 400 patients, but to treat 800 patients per month, an additional exam and treatment room would be needed. Also, adding exam and treatment rooms would mean that the business would need additional treatment equipment.

In looking deeper at the expenses of Uptown Chiropractic, Dr. Press concluded that even though some expenses would increase if he expanded the business, not all his expenses would increase, and therefore, he hoped the business would be more profitable.

For example, while it would cost more to expand the office to add an exam and treatment room, the existing office and waiting area wouldn't have to be enlarged, and the business could more fully use the existing treatment rooms. Additionally, the senior chiropractic assistant's time could be spread out over more patients and used more effectively, so only a junior chiropractic assistant would need to be added to staff.

The "Costs of Expansion" chart (below) shows Dr. Press' analysis of the costs of adding another doctor and doubling the number of patients treated.

In the office's first year, the cost of services and the general and administrative expenses of the business total $21,500 per month, a cost per treatment of $54. Dr. Press' analysis indicates that doubling the number of patients treated will only cost an additional $15,000 per month. The total cost of treating 800 patients per month would be $36,500, a cost per treatment of $46.

Uptown Chiropractic Costs of Expansion	First Year Costs	Additional Costs	Costs when Expanded to Two Doctors
Number of Treatments per Month	400	400	800
Cost of Services			
Dr. Press' Salary	$5,000		$5,000
Second Chiropractor		$5,000	$5,000
Sr. Chiropractic Assistant	$2,500		$2,500
Jr. Chiropractic Assistant	$2,000	$2,000	$4,000
Treatment Supplies	$2,000	$2,000	$4,000
Total Cost of Services	**$11,500**	**$9,000**	**$20,500**
General and Administrative			
Rent	$2,000	$1,000	$3,000
Utilities	$1,000	$500	$1,500
Equipment Lease	$4,500	$3,000	$7,500
Bookkeeper/Billing Clerk	$1,500	$1,500	$3,000
Licenses, Certifications, Training	$500		$500
Accounting, Payroll and Legal	$500		$500
Total General and Administrative	**$10,000**	**$6,000**	**$16,000**
Total Expenses	**$21,500**	**$15,000**	**$36,500**
Cost per Treatment	**$54**		**$46**

Dr. Press concluded that the business could treat twice as many patients without incurring twice as many costs, and therefore, the business should be more profitable if it expands.

Next, Dr. Press looked at the how the cash flow of the business would be affected by an expansion. He was well aware that it took the insurance companies 120 days to pay, and that if the business expanded, Uptown Chiropractic would need to pay these increased expenses while waiting for payment from the insurance companies.

The "Growth in Patient Treatments" chart (below) shows the projected number of patient treatments to be provided from January through June 2010, as well as the insurance company reimbursement, assuming the number of patient treatments doubled, beginning in January 2010.

Uptown Chiropractic
Growth in Patient Treatments

	Jan. 2010	Feb. 2010	Mar. 2010	April 2010	May 2010	June 2010
Patient Treatments	800	800	800	800	800	800
Patient Treatments Paid in Cash	200	200	200	200	200	200
Patient Treatments Submitted to Insurance	600	600	600	600	600	600
Insurance Reimbursement for Patient Treatments	300	300	300	600	600	600

Although the number of patient treatments has doubled, it will take some time for the insurance company reimbursement payments to catch up. During January, February and March, the insurance company payments still reflect the lower number of patient treatments. It's not until April that Uptown Chiropractic begins to receive reimbursement for the increased number of treatments.

The effect of this can be seen very clearly in the chart titled "Growth Projection Without Additional Cash" (see page 254). During January, February and March, Uptown Chiropractic has expanded its business and is paying increased operating and patient treatment expenses, but is not yet receiving payment for these treatments from the insurance companies.

Uptown Chiropractic Growth Projection Without Additional Cash

	Jan. 2010	Feb. 2010	Mar. 2010	April 2010	May 2010	June 2010
Cash Received						
Cash from Financing Activities						
Owners' Investment						
Bank Financing						
Total Cash from Financing Activities	$0	$0	$0	$0	$0	$0
Cash from Operating Activities						
Revenue						
Cash Payments	$15,000	$15,000	$15,000	$15,000	$15,000	$15,000
Insurance Reimbursement	$16,500	$16,500	$16,500	$33,000	$33,000	$33,000
Total Cash from Operating Activities	**$31,500**	**$31,500**	**$31,500**	**$48,000**	**$48,000**	**$48,000**
Total Cash Received	**$31,500**	**$31,500**	**$31,500**	**$48,000**	**$48,000**	**$48,000**
Cash Paid						
Cash Used for Asset Activities						
Startup Expenses						
Furniture and Fixtures						
Computer Equipment						
Total Cash Used for Asset Activities						
Cash Used in Operating Activities						
Cost of Services						
Doctors' Salaries	$10,000	$10,000	$10,000	$10,000	$10,000	$10,000
Sr. Chiropractic Assistant	$2,500	$2,500	$2,500	$2,500	$2,500	$2,500
Jr. Chiropractic Assistant	$4,000	$4,000	$4,000	$4,000	$4,000	$4,000
Treatment Supplies	$4,000	$4,000	$4,000	$4,000	$4,000	$4,000
General and Administrative						
Rent	$3,000	$3,000	$3,000	$3,000	$3,000	$3,000
Utilities	$1,500	$1,500	$1,500	$1,500	$1,500	$1,500
Equipment Lease	$7,000	$7,000	$7,000	$7,000	$7,000	$7,000
Bookkeeper/ Billing Clerk	$3,000	$3,000	$3,000	$3,000	$3,000	$3,000
Licenses, Certifications, Training	$500	$500	$500	$500	$500	$500
Accounting, Payroll and Legal	$500	$500	$500	$500	$500	$500
Interest Paid	$400	$400	$400	$400	$400	$400
Income Taxes Paid	$4,031	$4,031	$4,031	$4,031	$4,031	$4,031
Total Cash Used in Operating Activities						
Total Cash Paid	**$40,431**	**$40,431**	**$40,431**	**$40,431**	**$40,431**	**$40,431**
Net Cash Flow	**($8,931)**	**($8,931)**	**($8,931)**	**$7,569**	**$7,569**	**$7,569**
Beginning of Period Cash	$13,230	$4,299	($4,632)	($13,562)	($5,993)	$1,576
Plus Net Cash Flow	($8,931)	($8,931)	($8,931)	$7,569	$7,569	$7,569
End of Period Cash	**$4,299**	**($4,632)**	**($13,562)**	**($5,993)**	**$1,576**	**$9,145**

During each of these months, the business is projected to spend $8,931 more cash than it takes in. Over the course of three months, the business will spend $26,793 more cash than it takes in.

As we saw in the "First Year Cash Flow Statement" (on page 249), Uptown Chiropractic ended the prior year with $13,230 in cash. In order to expand the business and be able to survive for three months until the insurance reimbursement starts coming in, the business will need more cash—at least an additional $13,562.

Although the growth of the business is expected to result in increased profitability, it will also require additional cash. If the business doesn't have access to additional cash, it won't be able to expand.

Growing a BUSINESS takes MONEY.

Conversely, if Uptown Chiropractic expands without realizing that it needs additional cash and without a means to access more cash, it will go broke before it's able to generate the needed profits from its growth.

Recognizing this, Dr. Press believes it would be prudent to obtain $18,000 in additional bank financing to fund the business's cash needs during expansion. The expansion of Uptown Chiropractic is expected to result in increased profitability so the funds may not be needed for an extended period of time, but they clearly will be necessary to pay the bills during the first few months after the business grows.

The chart on page 256 ("Growth Projection With Additional Cash") shows a cash flow projection for Uptown Chiropractic that assumes the business borrows an additional $18,000. The business has a positive end of period cash balance in the months between January and June 2010.

In April, the insurance companies begin reimbursing Uptown Chiropractic for the increased number of patient treatments and the business starts generating more than $7,400 in positive cash flow each month. This cash might well be used to begin paying down some of the business's bank loans.

Uptown Chiropractic Growth Projection With Additional Cash

	Jan. 2010	Feb. 2010	Mar. 2010	April 2010	May 2010	June 2010
Cash Received						
Cash from Financing Activities						
Owners' Investment						
Bank Financing	$18,000					
Total Cash from Financing Activities	**$18,000**	**$0**	**$0**	**$0**	**$0**	**$0**
Cash from Operating Activities						
Revenue						
Cash Payments	$15,000	$15,000	$15,000	$15,000	$15,000	$15,000
Insurance Reimbursement	$16,500	$16,500	$16,500	$33,000	$33,000	$33,000
Total Cash from Operating Activities	**$31,500**	**$31,500**	**$31,500**	**$48,000**	**$48,000**	**$48,000**
Total Cash Received	**$49,500**	**$31,500**	**$31,500**	**$48,000**	**$48,000**	**$48,000**
Cash Paid						
Cash Used for Asset Activities						
Startup Expenses						
Furniture and Fixtures						
Computer Equipment						
Total Cash Used for Asset Activities	**$0**	**$0**	**$0**	**$0**	**$0**	**$0**
Cash Used in Operating Activities						
Cost of Services						
Doctors' Salaries	$10,000	$10,000	$10,000	$10,000	$10,000	$10,000
Sr. Chiropractic Assistant	$2,500	$2,500	$2,500	$2,500	$2,500	$2,500
Jr. Chiropractic Assistant	$4,000	$4,000	$4,000	$4,000	$4,000	$4,000
Treatment Supplies	$4,000	$4,000	$4,000	$4,000	$4,000	$4,000
General and Administrative						
Rent	$3,000	$3,000	$3,000	$3,000	$3,000	$3,000
Utilities	$1,500	$1,500	$1,500	$1,500	$1,500	$1,500
Equipment Lease	$7,000	$7,000	$7,000	$7,000	$7,000	$7,000
Bookkeeper/ Billing Clerk	$3,000	$3,000	$3,000	$3,000	$3,000	$3,000
Licenses, Certifications, Training	$500	$500	$500	$500	$500	$500
Accounting, Payroll and Legal	$500	$500	$500	$500	$500	$500
Interest Paid	$600	$600	$600	$600	$600	$600
Income Taxes Paid	$3,961	$3,961	$3,961	$3,961	$3,961	$3,961
Total Cash Used in Operating Activities	**$40,561**	**$40,561**	**$40,561**	**$40,561**	**$40,561**	**$40,561**
Total Cash Paid	**$40,461**	**$40,461**	**$40,461**	**$40,461**	**$40,461**	**$40,461**
Net Cash Flow	**$8,939**	**($9,061)**	**($9,061)**	**$7,439**	**$7,439**	**$7,439**
Beginning of Period Cash	**$13,230**	**$22,169**	**$13,108**	**$4,048**	**$11,487**	**$18,926**
Plus Net Cash Flow	$8,939	($9,061)	($9,061)	$7,439	$7,439	$7,439
End of Period Cash	**$22,169**	**$13,108**	**$4,048**	**$11,487**	**$18,926**	**$26,365**

Finally, let's look at the profit and loss statement and balance sheet for Uptown Chiropractic. Charts for the projected profit and loss statement for the first six months of 2010 and the balance sheet as of June 30, 2010 are on pages 257 and 258, respectively.

Uptown Chiropractic
Projected Profit and Loss Statement
January – June 2010

	Jan. 2010	Feb. 2010	Mar. 2010	April 2010	May 2010	June 2010
Sales Activities						
Revenue	$48,000	$48,000	$48,000	$48,000	$48,000	$48,000
Cost of Goods Sold	$20,500	$20,500	$20,500	$20,500	$20,500	$20,500
Gross Profit	$27,500	$27,500	$27,500	$27,500	$27,500	$27,500
Operating Expenses						
General and Administrative	$15,500	$15,500	$15,500	$15,500	$15,500	$15,500
Depreciation	$83	$83	$83	$83	$83	$83
Total Operating Expenses	$15,583	$15,583	$15,583	$15,583	$15,583	$15,583
Operating Profit	$11,917	$11,917	$11,917	$11,917	$11,917	$11,917
Interest	$600	$600	$600	$600	$600	$600
Profit Before Taxes	$11,317	$11,317	$11,317	$11,317	$11,317	$11,317
Income Taxes @ 35%	$3,961	$3,961	$3,961	$3,961	$3,961	$3,961
Net Profit	$7,356	$7,356	$7,356	$7,356	$7,356	$7,356

The business is indeed projected to be more profitable. Treating 400 patients per month, the business earned a net profit of $15,730 for the year. By hiring additional staff and expanding the business to allow the 800 patient treatments per month, Uptown Chiropractic is projected to become much more profitable. The business is projected to earn $7,356 per month, for a total net profit of $88,272 for the year.

Uptown Chiropractic
Projected Balance Sheet
June 30, 2010

Assets
  Current Assets

Cash	$26,365
Accounts Receivable	$99,000
Inventory	$0
Total Current Assets	**$125,365**

  Plant, Property and Equipment

Equipment	$10,000
Less: Accumulated Depreciation	($1,500)
Total Plant, Property and Equipment	**$8,500**

Total Assets	**$133,865**

Liabilities and Owners' Equity
Liabilities
  Current Liabilities

Accounts Payable	$0
Total Current Liabilities	**$0**

  Long-Term Liabilities

Loan from Bank	$54,000
Total Long-Term Liabilities	**$54,000**

Total Liabilities	**$54,000**

Owners' Equity

Owners' Investment	$20,000
Retained Earnings	$59,865
Total Owners' Equity	**$79,865**

Total Liabilities and Owners' Equity	**$133,865**

The growth of Uptown Chiropractic will also result in an increase in the size of the balance sheet. Total assets will grow from $71,730 to $133,865. Unfortunately, most of this asset growth will occur in accounts receivable. As a result of doubling the number of patient treatments each month, the size of the business's accounts receivable—reimbursement due from insurance companies for treatments provided—will also double, from $49,500 to $99,000. The working capital invested in the business will now be $99,000.

How Fast Should You Grow?

As you can see by this example, growing a business takes money. In our example, Uptown Chiropractic needed additional cash to grow that would allow it to pays bills while waiting for payment from the insurance companies.

The same would be true for almost any business. A consulting business that landed a big contract and hired staff to help with the extra work would need cash to pay the new employees while awaiting payment from the client.

A retail business that expands an existing store would need extra cash to pay for its additional inventory. A retail chain that grows by opening stores would need more cash to pay for the setup of the new stores.

The expansion of a manufacturing business will often require cash for the purchase of additional manufacturing equipment and for raw materials to be used in the production process as well as for the hiring of additional staff.

How much money a business needs to grow depends on the amount of working capital used in the business, the cash collection cycle, and the additional operating or capital expenses of the expansion.

For any business, there are three possible sources of money for growth. The business can receive additional investment from its owners, borrow the money, or use the money it's generated from operations.

A business that wants to grow rapidly and isn't generating sufficient cash from its operations will need to either borrow the money for growth or receive additional equity investment from its owners. If a business borrows money, there's some risk. The business will incur additional expenses associated with paying back the loan, and the growth or expansion will have to generate sufficient cash to allow the loan payments to be made.

Many businesses chose to grow more slowly, relying on the money the business is able to generate from its operations. In our Uptown Chiropractic example, in order to double the number of patient treatments, the business needed at least $13,562. We assumed the business borrowed $18,000, just so there was always a bit of cash in the bank as a contingency. This allowed the business to expand during its second year.

Many BUSINESSES choose
to grow more slowly.

But what if the business had been more conservative and wanted to grow only using the money it was able to generate from its operations? During its first year, Uptown Chiropractic's operating cash flow was negatively affected by the delay in receiving reimbursements from the insurance companies. The net cash flow of the business was only positive because of the receipt of a bank loan and the owner's investment.

In the second year, the operating cash flow is expected to turn positive. Once insurance company reimbursements are being received throughout the year, the business is expected to generate $16,730 in cash from operations each year.

Assuming the business would also be able to generate this same amount of cash in each of the subsequent years, it would be sometime toward the middle of the third year before the business can generate sufficient cash from operations to allow it to expand without borrowing or additional investment.

How quickly or slowly a business is able to expand is a function of the amount of cash the business is generating from operations, coupled with the tolerance the owners have for debt and their willingness to borrow to expand the business.

CHAPTER NINETEEN

Taxes and Your Business

There's an old saying that nothing in life is certain but death and taxes. As the owner or manager of a business, you'll certainly become familiar with taxes.

There are generally three types of taxes that a business must pay: income taxes, payroll taxes, and sales taxes. Let's look at each of these categories individually.

Income Taxes

In the United States, the federal government taxes the profits of businesses at rates that can be as high as 35 percent. In other words, if the business makes $100 of profit, $35 of that money must be paid to the federal government in the form of corporate income taxes.

Additionally, most states also tax the profits of corporations. These tax rates can run as high as 10 percent, although in many instances the effective tax rates are closer to 5 percent. If a business makes $100 of profit, in addition to paying $35 in taxes to the federal government, the corporation also has to pay between $5 and $10 in taxes to the state government.

It's important as a business owner or manager that you recognize the existence of these taxes and set aside money to pay them.

As you might expect, corporate income taxes can be complicated. While it's not the intent of this book to provide a detailed overview of corporate income taxes or the impact of your corporate structure on your personal income taxes, you should be aware that the federal and state governments will tax your business, and that the taxes need to be paid. You should consult with your accountant on your specific tax issues.

Accounting Rules Vs. Tax Rules

The first thing to know about taxes is that the rules of accounting and the rules of taxes are sometimes different. It's important that you understand how the profits of your business as reflected on your profit and loss statement can be different than the profits you report to the IRS for tax purposes. These variations result from the differences in tax and accounting rules for treatment of revenue and expenses.

One of the key differences between accounting and tax rules is the treatment of certain travel expenses, specifically meal and entertainment expenses.

If you or your employees will be traveling for business purposes or will be entertaining clients, this difference should be of interest to you. Under IRS regulations, a business is only allowed to deduct for tax purposes 50 percent of the cost of meal and entertainment expenses. If you take an overnight business trip to another city to meet with clients or to attend a conference, and spend $100 to eat while you're at the conference, accounting rules allow you to deduct the entire $100 on your profit and loss statement. However, IRS rules only allow you to deduct 50 percent of this $100, or $50, as an expense. This means that your business will appear to be $50 more profitable to the IRS than your profit and loss statement shows it to be. You'll be required to pay taxes on this additional $50 of profit.

While this may seem like a silly rule, it was created a number of years ago in reaction to the so-called "three martini lunches" that Congress perceived many businessmen were expensing.

When a business purchases an ASSET, it's required to DEPRECIATE the asset over the useful life defined by the IRS.

If you or your employees travel a significant amount for business purposes (such as meeting with clients, sales and marketing trips, making presentations, or attending conferences), this rule can result in a rather large difference between your accounting profits and your tax profits. It's important that you're aware of this rule so you're not surprised at tax time.

Another difference between your accounting profit and loss statement and your profits for purposes of taxes is the treatment of any federal income tax payments you make. Federal income tax payments made by the business are considered expenses for purposes of your profit and loss statement and are deducted prior to calculating your net profit. For tax purposes, federal income tax payments aren't a deductible expense. Therefore, the IRS will consider your net profit to be higher by the amount of your federal income tax payments and will base the amount of tax you owe on this higher net profit.

Depreciation

A second income tax consideration for business is depreciation. In Chapter 5, we discussed depreciation on the profit and loss statement. Depreciation allows a business to deduct the periodic wear and tear on equipment and machinery as an expense on the profit and loss statement.

As we described briefly in "Depreciation FAQs" in Chapter 7, the IRS has established rules regarding the useful life of various types of assets. These rules standardize the useful life a business must assume in depreciating assets.

Typically, when a business purchases an asset, it's required to depreciate the asset over the useful life defined by the IRS, using one of the approved depreciation methods. In general, a business can depreciate an asset using either a straight-line depreciation method or an accelerated depreciation method.

The IRS and state governments take PAYROLL TAXES very seriously.

When using a straight-line depreciation method, a business will depreciate the asset an equal amount each year. For example, if a business purchases a piece of machinery for $10,000 that has a useful life of five years, the business would depreciate one-fifth of this $10,000, or $2,000, each year for five years.

Alternatively, the business could use an accelerated depreciation method to depreciate this asset. An accelerated depreciation method allows the business to recognize more depreciation in the early years and less in later years.

If the business purchased the same $10,000 piece of machinery with a five-year useful life and used an accelerated depreciation method, it might be able to depreciate the asset $4,000 in the first year rather than $2,000. In the second year, it might depreciate the asset $2,400 instead of $2,000. But by the third year, it would only be able to depreciate the asset by $1,600 instead of $2,000, and in the final year, it would only be able to depreciate the remaining $800 of asset value instead of $2,000.

One final comment on depreciation: An asset's depreciation begins on the date the asset is acquired. If a business buys an asset early in the year, it's able to recognize more depreciation than if it purchases the asset later in the year.

SECTION 179 DEPRECIATION

To help small businesses, there's a section of the tax code known as section 179. Section 179 allows a business to depreciate the entire value of an asset in the year of purchase. This allows a small business to more closely match its cash flow with its profits.

For example, if a business purchased a computer and software for $10,000 cash and depreciated this computer over the five-year useful life defined by the IRS, the business might be able to deduct $2,000 per year as a depreciation expense. The business spent $10,000 to purchase the computer and yet is only able to deduct $2,000 as an expense. The section 179 option would allow the business to depreciate the entire $10,000 in the year of purchase, more closely aligning the cash outflow with the depreciation expense.

There are limitations on the types of assets that can be depreciated using section 179. Section 179 tends to be very useful for computers, software, machinery and equipment, and farm and agricultural assets, and less useful for automobiles and real estate assets.

The IRS also has an annual limit on the amount of section 179 depreciation a business can claim. Over the last few years, this limit has exceeded $100,000, which is more than adequate for a typical small business.

A business that purchases an asset and recognizes section 179 depreciation on the asset during the year of purchase can significantly reduce its taxable income and pay lower taxes for that year.

For instance, if a business purchases an asset on January 1, it will be able to depreciate that asset for the entire 12 months of the year. If a business purchases an asset on December 1, it will only be able to depreciate that asset for one month during that year.

Using our example from above, if a business purchased a $10,000 piece of equipment on December 1 that was eligible for $2,000 per year in depreciation, the business would only be able to recognize one-twelfth of the annual depreciation ($167) during the year of purchase, since there would only be one month remaining in the year. The remainder of the $2,000 annual depreciation will be recognized in the next calendar year.

For this reason, it's often beneficial for a business that plans to make substantial equipment purchases to wait until the beginning of the year to make those purchases so the business can get the full value of the depreciation in the year of purchase.

Payroll Taxes

In addition to income taxes, most businesses are also involved in collecting and remitting payroll taxes. When a business has employees, it's required to withhold certain taxes from employees' paychecks and pay the amounts withheld to the IRS, state tax agency, and Social Security Administration. It's also required to pay the employer share of Social Security and Medicare taxes.

Let's look at how this process works. The chart below shows the payroll withholding amounts for a typical employee. The gross pay for the employee is $1,000, but as we all know there's a difference between the amount you're paid and the amount you actually see on your check. The reason is the withholding of payroll taxes.

Payroll Withholding	
Gross Pay to Employee	$1,000
Employer Payroll Tax Withholding	
Federal Income Tax	$200
State Income Tax	$24
Social Security and Medicare	$76
Total Employer Payroll Tax Withholding	**$300**
Net Pay to Employee	**$700**

As you see in the chart, the employee's gross pay is $1,000, but there are several amounts withheld from the paycheck, including $200 for federal income tax, $24 for state income tax, and $76 for Social Security and Medicare. The employee receives $700; the total employer withholding is $300.

At the end of the month, the employer will be required to pay this $300 to the IRS, the state taxing agency, and the Social Security Administration. The business is acting as a tax collection agent for the government.

But wait, there's more. Employers are also required to make Social Security and Medicare tax payments on behalf of the employee. These payments aren't withheld from the employees' paychecks. Instead, they're made using the employer's money.

The "Payments to Taxing Agencies" chart (below) shows that in the example of our employee being paid $1,000, the employer must also contribute an additional 7.65 percent ($76 in this case) for the employer's share of Social Security and Medicare. In total, the employer must make a payment of $376 to the taxing agencies.

Payments to Taxing Agencies

Employer Payroll Tax Withholding	
Federal Income Tax	$200
State Income Tax	$24
Social Security and Medicare	$76
Total Employer Payroll Tax Withholding	**$300**
Employer Share of Social Security and Medicare	$76
Total Payment to Taxing Agencies	**$376**

The total cost of paying an employee $1,000 is shown in the chart below. The employee receives $700 and the employer withholds $300 of payroll taxes from the employee's pay on behalf of the taxing agencies. The employer is also obligated to pay a share of the Social Security and Medicare taxes ($76 in our example). In total, paying the employee $1,000 cost the business $1,076.

Total Cost of Paying Employee $1,000	
Net Pay to Employee	$700
Employer Payroll Tax Withholding	$300
Employer Share of Social Security and Medicare	$76
Total Cost of Paying Employee $1,000	**$1,076**

The IRS and state governments take payroll taxes very seriously. One of the quickest ways out of business is to withhold payroll taxes on behalf of your employees and not pay these taxes to the IRS, state tax department, or Social Security Administration. Not only is payment of these taxes required, it is often a personal obligation of the officers or owners of the business.

Sales Taxes

Most states impose a sales tax on the value of merchandise sold by retailers. In states that have a sales tax, the retailer acts as the tax collection agent for the state. If a retailer sells an item priced at $100 and the state has a 5-percent sales tax, the retailer will charge the customer $105 for the item. The retailer will keep $100 as its revenue from the sale and collect $5 on behalf of the state. At a later date, such as the end of the month or the end of the quarter, the retailer will pay the collected sales tax to the state.

As the owner or manager of a business that collects sales tax on behalf of the state, it's important to recognize that the business will need to have cash available to pay the sales tax to the state when it's due.

Additionally, it's important that the retailer understands which goods and services are taxable and which are not. In general, goods that are sold from a manufacturer or supplier to a retail store are not subject to sales tax. They become subject to sales tax at the time the retailer sells them.

However, not all merchandise is subject to sales tax. In many states, the food sold in supermarkets isn't subject to sales tax, although food purchased in a restaurant or convenience store might be.

Not paying taxes is a QUICK way out of business.

Likewise, some states apply sales tax to services provided by businesses. Professional organizations, such as consultants, accountants and attorneys, may find their services subject to sales tax.

Businesses are required to pay the sales tax to the state on taxable goods and services regardless of whether the business actually collected sales tax on that transaction. So it's critical that the business owner or manager makes sure they're collecting sales tax on goods and services subject to sales tax, or else they'll have to pay the tax from their profits.

While many businesses rely on accountants when it comes to tax issues, we can't stress enough the importance of the owner or manager understanding how taxes affect the financial statements and cash flows of the business. Ultimately, it's the owner or manager's responsibility to make sure the cash needed for tax payments is available and that the taxes get paid when due. Not paying taxes is a quick way out of business.

CHAPTER TWENTY

Accounting and Your Business

While this book is primarily about how to use the information on your financial statements to create and keep a profitable business, the accounting practices your company uses will play an important role in the creation of the financial statements and can affect your profitability.

In this chapter, we'll briefly discuss the role accounting software and systems play in a business today and the key differences between cash- and accrual-based accounting and how this choice can affect profitability. We'll also introduce the concept of an accounting fiscal year.

Fiscal Year

In most instances, when someone mentions a year, you think of the calendar year, the period from January 1 to December 31. But a year can actually run for any 365-day period. It's quite common in the business world to have events that last a year but don't run from January 1 to December 31.

For instance, your business might sign a contract to provide a service to another business for the next year. If you sign this contract on April 1, it will expire in one year, on March 31. Likewise, your business might sign a contract to purchase a service for the next year (such as a computer service contract or the contract with your cell phone provider). If you sign this contract on October 5, it will expire on October 4 of the following year.

The concept of a fiscal year is very simple: It's the one-year accounting period the business uses to record its profitability, create its balance sheet and pay its taxes.

A BUSINESS has the right to CHOOSE any 365-day period for its fiscal year that it feels is APPROPRIATE.

For most businesses, the fiscal year is the same as the calendar year. That is, the accounting period for the business runs from January 1 to December 31. The financial statements for the business are prepared using December 31 of each year as the end date.

But a business has the right to choose any 365-day period for its fiscal year that it feels is appropriate. In some industries, it makes more sense for a business to choose a date other than December 31 as the end date for its fiscal year.

For instance, many retailers have their fiscal year end on January 31 or February 28 because the Christmas season is their prime selling season. The majority of their annual sales occur during the final few months of the calendar year as customers purchase Christmas gifts for family and friends.

Immediately after Christmas, some of those Christmas gifts are returned. The sales the retailers thought they made in November or December are returned the last week of December or in early January. If the financial books are closed on December 31, the returns from early January won't be reflected, and the business risks overstating its revenue. Closing the books a month or two later gives the retailers the opportunity to record all the sales and returns from the Christmas season. These businesses select a fiscal year that makes sense given the selling cycle of their industries.

Another example might be businesses that sell goods or services to colleges or schools. The educational year for most colleges and schools runs from early fall until late spring. By May or June, the educational year is finished, and administrators are preparing for the next year. For businesses that provide goods and services to college and schools, a fiscal year that ends on June 30 or July 31 might make more sense than one ending on December 31.

By choosing to end their fiscal year on a date other than December 31, businesses with unique operating characteristics may be able to produce financial statements that more accurately reflect the events of the operating period. If the operating period for your business doesn't logically end on December 31, you should consider using a fiscal year that differs from the calendar year.

Cash and Accrual Accounting

As we mentioned briefly in Chapter 5, a business can account for its transactions using cash accounting or accrual accounting methodology.

Under cash accounting, the business recognizes all its accounting events when the cash is either received or paid. If a business sells a product or provides a service to a customer, the business records the revenue when the cash is actually received from the customer. If the business receives a bill from a supplier or service provider, and pays the bill in 30 days, the business records the expense in 30 days when the check is written.

Under accrual accounting, the business recognizes all its accounting events when they take place, regardless of when the cash is actually received. If the business sells a product or provides a service to the customer, the business must record the revenue when the product is sold or the service is provided, regardless of whether the customer pays at that time or at a future date. If the business receives products from a supplier or receives services from a service provider, the amount owed to the supplier or service provider is immediately recorded as an expense.

How should a business decide whether to use cash or accrual accounting? In many instances, a company's choice of accounting method will be dictated by the type and size of the business. Under tax rules in the United States, if the business produces, purchases or sells merchandise, the company must use the accrual method of accounting. The Internal Revenue Service code has an exception carved out for "qualifying small businesses," which are defined as those with annual gross receipts under $1 million.

If a business has inventory and is manufacturing or selling products, it will probably need to use accrual accounting. The exception for qualifying small businesses allows companies that sell limited amounts of products to continue to use cash accounting.

If the business PRODUCES, PURCHASES or SELLS merchandise, the business must use the ACCRUAL METHOD of ACCOUNTING.

Taxes are a complicated issue, and if your business is planning on using cash accounting and carrying inventory and manufacturing or selling products, we strongly urge you to consult with a professional tax advisor.

Of our three example companies, Bonnie's Beachwear and Boutique Handbags both sell or manufacture products and have inventory, and, therefore, would need to use accrual accounting. For our example in this chapter, we'll use Uptown Chiropractic. As a service business, Uptown Chiropractic will likely have little or no inventory and will be eligible to use either the cash or accrual method of accounting.

Let's see how the choice of accounting method affects the financial statements of Uptown Chiropractic.

As presented in Chapter 2, Uptown Chiropractic expects to treat 400 patients per month and receive an average payment of $55 per treatment from insurance companies and an average payment of $75 per treatment from patients who pay cash.

If 25 percent of Uptown Chiropractic's patients pay cash, the business will generate $90,000 per year from this patient group. If the remaining 75 percent of the patient treatments are reimbursed by insurance companies at $55 per treatment, Uptown Chiropractic can expect to generate $198,000 per year from this patient group.

As we described in Chapter 2, the insurance companies take 120 days to pay Uptown Chiropractic for treatments. This means that in the case of patient treatments where Uptown Chiropractic is paid by the insurance companies, there will be a difference between the number of patient treatments the business performs and the number of treatments for which it is paid.

During the first year of operations, Uptown Chiropractic will perform 1,200 patient treatments for cash customers and 3,600 patient treatments for insurance customers. Uptown Chiropractic will be paid for the 1,200 cash customer treatments at the time of service. However, because of the 120-day collection period for the insurance company reimbursements, Uptown Chiropractic will only be paid for 2,700 patient treatments during the first year. This means that instead of receiving $198,000 in cash for these patient treatments, the business will only receive $148,500. The remainder will be received in the next year.

We'll use this difference in cash receipts vs. patient treatments to demonstrate the difference between the cash and accrual accounting methods.

Accrual Accounting

Let's assume that Uptown Chiropractic uses the calendar year as its fiscal year and began operations on January 1, 2009.

On its first-year cash flow statement (see page 277), we see that Uptown Chiropractic received $238,500 in cash from operating activities during the year. We also see that the business paid out $271,270 for operating activities and $10,000 in startup expenses, spending more cash than it received from operating activities. The net cash flow of the business is positive only because of financing activities—the investment by the owner and the receipt of bank financing.

Uptown Chiropractic
First-Year Cash Flow Statement
Accrual Basis

Year Ending
Dec. 31, 2009

Cash Received	
Cash from Financing Activities	
Owners' Investment	$20,000
Bank Financing	$36,000
Total Cash from Financing Activities	**$56,000**
Cash from Operating Activities	
Revenue	
Cash Payments	$90,000
Insurance Reimbursement	$148,500
Total Cash from Operating Activities	**$238,500**
Total Cash Received	**$294,500**
Cash Paid	
Cash Used for Asset Activities	
Startup Expenses	
Furniture and Fixtures	$5,000
Computer Equipment	$5,000
Total Cash Used for Asset Activities	**$10,000**
Cash Used in Operating Activities	
Cost of Services	
Doctor's Salary	$60,000
Sr. Chiropractic Assistant	$30,000
Jr. Chiropractic Assistant	$24,000
Treatment Supplies	$24,000
General and Administrative	
Rent	$24,000
Utilities	$12,000
Equipment Lease	$54,000
Bookkeeper/Billing Clerk	$18,000
Licenses, Certifications,Training	$6,000
Accounting, Payroll and Legal	$6,000
Interest Paid	$4,800
Income Taxes Paid	$8,470
Total Cash Used in Operating Activities	**$271,270**
Total Cash Paid	**$281,270**
Net Cash Flow	**$13,230**
Beginning of Period Cash	**$0**
Plus Net Cash Flow	$13,230
End of Period Cash	**$13,230**

Next let's look at the first-year profit and loss statement for Uptown Chiropractic prepared using accrual accounting. Under the rules of accrual accounting, Uptown Chiropractic must recognize the revenues for its patient treatments at the time services are provided rather than when the cash is received.

OWNERS and MANAGERS need to understand...how accounting decisions can AFFECT the company.

The chart on page 279 provides Uptown Chiropractic's first-year profit and loss statement prepared using accrual accounting. For purposes of the profit and loss statement, the revenue of the business during the year was $288,000.

The business generated an operating profit of $29,000, earnings before taxes were $24,200, and because the business made a profit, it will owe $8,470 in income taxes.

Uptown Chiropractic
First-Year Profit and Loss Statement
Accrual Basis

Year Ending
Dec. 31, 2009

Sales Activities	
Revenue	$288,000
Cost of Services	
Doctor's Salary	$60,000
Assistants' Salaries	$54,000
Treatment Supplies	$24,000
Total Cost of Services	$138,000
Gross Profit	**$150,000**
Operating Expenses	
General and Administrative	
Rent	$24,000
Utilities	$12,000
Equipment Lease	$54,000
Bookkeeper/Billing Clerk	$18,000
Licenses, Certifications, Training	$6,000
Accounting, Payroll and Legal	$6,000
Total General and Administrative	$120,000
Depreciation	$1,000
Total Operating Expenses	$121,000
Operating Profit	**$29,000**
Interest	$4,800
Profit before Taxes	**$24,200**
Income Taxes @ 35%	$8,470
Net Profit	**$15,730**

Let's look at the profit and taxes a bit more closely. Even though the business used more cash in operating activities than it took in, using the accrual accounting method, it made a profit. And since it made a profit, it owes income taxes. A closer look at the cash flow statement on page 277 shows the business used some of its cash to pay $8,470 in income taxes.

Cash Accounting

Now let's look at the first-year profit and loss statement for Uptown Chiropractic prepared using the cash accounting method.

The chart on page 281 shows Uptown Chiropractic's first-year profit and loss statement prepared under the rules of cash accounting. Using cash accounting, Uptown Chiropractic recognizes revenue for the patient treatments it provides at the time they're paid for. That is, when it receives the cash. Since the business only received $238,500 in cash for patient treatments during the year, the revenue is $238,500.

The operating profit of the business is negative, as are earnings before taxes. Since the business lost money during the year, no income taxes are due.

Uptown Chiropractic
First-Year Profit and Loss Statement
Cash Basis

	Year Ending Dec. 31, 2009
Sales Activities	
Revenue	$238,500
Cost of Services	
Doctor's Salary	$60,000
Assistants' Salaries	$54,000
Treatment Supplies	$24,000
Total Cost of Services	$138,000
Gross Profit	**$100,500**
Operating Expenses	
General and Administrative	
Rent	$24,000
Utilities	$12,000
Equipment Lease	$54,000
Bookkeeper/Billing Clerk	$18,000
Licenses, Certifications, Training	$6,000
Accounting, Payroll and Legal	$6,000
Total General and Administrative	$120,000
Depreciation	$1,000
Total Operating Expenses	$121,000
Operating Profit	**($20,500)**
Interest	$4,800
Profit before Taxes	**($25,300)**
Income Taxes @ 35%	$0
Net Profit	**($25,300)**

The chart on page 282 shows the cash flow statement for the first year of operations of Uptown Chiropractic, assuming the business used the cash accounting method. The cash flows are exactly the same as under the accrual accounting method, except the business didn't pay any income taxes, so it ends the period with $21,700 in cash vs. the $13,230 it had when using accrual accounting.

Uptown Chiropractic
First-Year Cash Flow Statement
Cash Basis

Year Ending
Dec. 31, 2009

Cash Received	
Cash from Financing Activities	
Owners' Investment	$20,000
Bank Financing	$36,000
Total Cash from Financing Activities	**$56,000**
Cash from Operating Activities	
Revenue	
Cash Payments	$90,000
Insurance Reimbursement	$148,500
Total Cash from Operating Activities	**$238,500**
Total Cash Received	**$294,500**
Cash Paid	
Cash Used for Asset Activities	
Startup Expenses	
Furniture and Fixtures	$5,000
Computer Equipment	$5,000
Total Cash Used for Asset Activities	**$10,000**
Cash Used in Operating Activities	
Cost of Services	
Doctor's Salary	$60,000
Sr. Chiropractic Assistant	$30,000
Jr. Chiropractic Assistant	$24,000
Treatment Supplies	$24,000
General and Administrative	
Rent	$24,000
Utilities	$12,000
Equipment Lease	$54,000
Bookkeeper/Billing Clerk	$18,000
Licenses, Certifications,Training	$6,000
Accounting, Payroll and Legal	$6,000
Interest Paid	$4,800
Income Taxes Paid	$0
Total Cash Used in Operating Activities	**$262,800**
Total Cash Paid	**$272,800**
Net Cash Flow	**$21,700**
Beginning of Period Cash	**$0**
Plus Net Cash Flow	$21,700
End of Period Cash	**$21,700**

As this example demonstrates, it may be advantageous for Uptown Chiropractic to use the cash accounting method instead of the accrual accounting method.

When using accrual accounting, the business is generating profits and a tax liability on an accounting profit where it has not yet received the cash, and Uptown Chiropractic must use some of its own cash (in this case, obtained from the owner's investment and the bank loan) to pay its taxes.

As the business grows and there continues to be delay between the treatment of patients and the receipt of cash, the use of the cash accounting method allows Uptown Chiropractic to most closely match its cash revenue and expenses with its accounting revenue and expenses. Its tax liabilities will be based on the cash it actually received and spent, which will help reduce the cash needed by the business to operate.

Accounting Software and Systems

Unless your business has been formed to provide accounting services or accounting software, or you like to wear green eyeshades and make ledger entries in the middle of the night, you'll probably hire someone or buy some software to help you with your accounting.

Many small businesses today use inexpensive computer software programs such as QuickBooks or Peachtree to handle the day-to-day accounting, and contract with service providers to handle the more complicated tasks of managing employees and payroll. A complete list of accounting software providers can be found on our website www.FinanceWithoutFear.com.

These software packages provide full-service accounting functionality for most businesses. They allow a business to enter inventory purchases, create customer invoices and billing statements, track accounts receivable, receive payments, track accounts payable and pay bills. They also will print checks, help keep the bank statements in balance, and provide full financial statement reporting.

Many of these software packages come with prepackaged templates that create different charts of accounts for various types of businesses. The template for a professional services provider will be different from that for a manufacturer or a retailer. The template will include those particular assets, liabilities and other accounts that are typical to that particular type of business.

While accounting software has replaced many of the manual roles a bookkeeper or accountant formerly performed such as preparing financial reports or adding columns of numbers on a calculator, many businesses still employ bookkeepers and accountants to process transactions using accounting software. This frees the business owner or manager to focus on operating the business to make money.

Owners and managers need to understand the financial statements and how accounting decisions can affect the company, but they can typically be more useful to the business when focused on strategic and operational issues (such as how to make money) rather than entering transactions into the accounting system.

CHAPTER TWENTY-ONE

Finding Money to Start and Operate Your Business

 A key part of starting any business is determining the source of the money needed to launch the business. The money used to start a business is typically referred to as startup capital.

There are four main sources of startup capital for a business:

1. Your money
2. Family and friends
3. Small-business lenders
4. Outside investors and venture capitalists

We'll discuss each of these individually. Let's start by looking at your money.

Your Money

In almost all instances, the owner's own money is the initial source of capital for a new business. If possible, it's best that you start your business using entirely your own money. This way, you don't have to spend time explaining to others how the business is going to make money and how you intend to repay them. You still need to understand how the business is going to make money, but it won't be necessary to create a lot of documentation to explain it to others.

Typically, an owner's personal funds come either from savings, retirement accounts, equity in his/her house, or personal credit cards.

Your savings accounts are easiest to access and should be looked at first. You could use retirement funds, but these are often only available to you with taxes to be paid and early withdrawal penalties. And, of course, you're eating up the money you need for your retirement.

You could turn to the equity in your home through a mortgage refinancing or home equity loan or line of credit. These loans tend to have relatively low interest rates but carry the risk of losing your home if the loan can't be repaid.

Credit cards are a common source of startup funding but generally carry high interest rates and tricky provisions that can make them a very expensive way to borrow. Many startup businesses have been funded using cash advances from the owner's credit cards.

Family and Friends

The second best option for funding your startup business is to turn to your family and friends. One of the advantages of obtaining startup financing from family and friends is they understand your work ethic and are often willing to invest in your business based on this and the strength of your character, without forcing you through the same underwriting process a professional lender would use.

If the business doesn't go as expected, family members are likely to be the most understanding or forgiving of an extended payback because they'll have strong ties to you beyond the loan they gave you. Of course, if things go poorly, you run the risk of having family members who will never talk to you again because your business failed and you didn't pay them back.

Friends are the next best source of funding and have some of the same positives as family members. Friends are likely to be somewhat understanding if things go badly and your payback becomes extended. However, as with family members, you're at the risk of losing a friend if the money they lend you is lost, and you're never able to pay them back.

As a business owner, you should make sure the lenders (your family and friends) fully understand the risk of their loan or investment. If not, you risk that your lenders or investors will suddenly wake up and demand payment, which could be very disruptive for the business.

Small-Business Lenders

Your own money and the investment from your family and friends may not be enough to fully fund your business startup. When this happens, you'll need to look to a small-business lender or investor for the additional money.

The next most likely source of funds is a loan from a lending institution. Typical small-business lenders include banks and credit unions as well as community loan funds.

How Lenders Look at Borrowers

Let's first talk about the training and philosophy of people who lend money to others for a living. In any borrowing situation, the lender is going to want a very solid reason to believe you'll pay back the loan according to the terms you've agreed upon. In evaluating loan applications, all lenders are taught to focus on the three C's of credit: character, capacity and collateral.

1. Character: This helps lenders determine if you're going to pay back the money they lend you, with interest and on time. In general, people who have a history of paying their loans on time keep paying on time. Correspondingly, people who have a history of being late or not paying off their loans tend to do that same thing again and again.

The credit report is an important part of what lenders look at when determining your character. It shows a couple of years of payment history on the loans you've had recently. It also has information on loan charge-offs and bankruptcies.

Today, most lenders use the credit score number on the credit report as a significant indicator of whether or not you will repay your loan. The credit score ranges from a high of 850 (fantastic) to a low of 300 (awful). Every lender uses its own cutoffs and segments. The chart below shows some typical ranges:

How Lenders View Credit Scores

Credit Score	Evaluation
730+	Great
690 to 730	Very Good
650 to 690	Good
620 to 650	OK
550 to 620	Poor
300 to 550	Awful

Even if you've incorporated your company, the lender may still look at your personal credit history. Since a new business doesn't have an established credit history, the lender must look someplace else to establish the character of the business, and that is the owner's credit history.

2. *Capacity:* Does the business have a realistic and dependable way to get the money to make the loan payments over time? In a business, this is largely a cash flow issue. You'll need to be able to show that the business can generate the necessary cash to make its loan payments over the term of the loan.

3. *Collateral:* Lenders want to know that you have assets that can be used as a backup source of payment if the business isn't generating the cash flow necessary to repay the loan. These assets could include personal savings, investments, retirement accounts, cash value of insurance policies, home equity, business assets, and anything else that could be easily sold to generate cash. If some of these items seem draconian to you, you must understand that the lender expects you to do whatever is necessary to make the loan payments.

In addition to the three C's, you need to build a relationship with the lender. In some ways, once the loan is made, you're partners. As such, never let the lender be surprised with bad news, and never lie or mislead the lender.

Remember that when negotiating a loan, lenders aren't your friends, coaches, or guardian angels. They're other businesspeople working on a transaction that will give their organization a financial return on the money they lend to you. They expect you to be able to pay the loan back, with interest. Lenders want a mutually beneficial relationship that will make them look good because you always pay your loan on time, and you'll come back to borrow more money in the future.

If your business is borrowing from a bank, credit union or community loan fund, it's very typical that the lender will charge you an interest rate that is between 5 and 15 percent. These rates compensate lenders for the risk they're taking in lending money to small and startup businesses. For instance, in the case examples in this book, we've assumed that our sample companies are paying interest rates of 10 and 12 percent on their bank loans.

TYPICAL BUSINESS PLAN ELEMENTS

A business plan is a document that outlines a business's operating and financial strategy. A business plan defines the structure of the business, identifies the products and services it intends to offer, defines the operating strategies the business will use, and identifies how it will make money.

A typical business plan includes seven major sections:

1. *Executive summary:* The executive summary outlines the content of the business plan. It includes the business's key strengths, identifies how much money is needed and for how long, and projects how the business will repay the loan. The executive summary is best kept brief, generally no more than one or two pages.

2. *Company organization and owner background:* The business plan should describe the legal form of the company, the capabilities and experience of the owner and other key employees, the staff organization, and the major facilities and equipment to be used.

3. *Product and services:* This section should describe the products and services to be produced and sold, including a categorization, if appropriate, by product type and price, with sales projections.

4. *Market analysis:* Here's where the competitive advantage of the business is addressed as well as the market segments that will be covered by each product or service the business offers. The advantages your products and services will have over those currently on the market should be discussed, in addition to the marketing, advertising and selling activities planned.

5. *Competitive analysis:* This section should explain your business strategy and the source of your competitive advantage. It should also identify major competitors, describe their strengths and weaknesses, and discuss how you'll maintain your competitive edge against them. In addition, you'll describe the local economy and how its current composition and expected changes will affect the business as well as review any technological or regulatory trends likely to have an impact.

6. *Operating plan:* The operating section explains how the business will produce and deliver products and services using facilities, equipment, technology, suppliers and labor, including a breakdown of the labor, materials and overhead costs. This section should also discuss the sources and adequacy of startup capital. It's particularly important to address how likely the business is to need more capital in the future.

7. *Three years of financial statements:* The cash flow statement, profit and loss statement, and balance sheets should show the most likely forecast for the business and include the critical ratios and other industry standard benchmarks for the business. For a startup business, these can be projected financial statements. For an existing business, you should include the business's actual financial statements.

Our companion workbook, the *Finance Without Fear Business Forecasting Workbook*, describes how to develop financial projections for your business.

Business plans can be relatively brief or long, depending on the complexity of the business and the expectations of the lender. You might ask your lender what he/she wants to see in the plan and then create the document with that lender in mind. You'll find additional information on how to create a business plan on our website www.FinanceWithoutFear.com.

Writing the business plan can be a great way to think through the viability of the venture and identify its danger points. Creating the financial projections will also force you to look at the financial operations of the business and identify the sources of startup and operating capital so you can determine how much money will be needed to start and operate the business.

How Lenders Look at Your Business

Once you've decided to try to get a loan to finance your startup or growing business, your job is to convince the lender that you're a good credit risk. This means you'll be able to pay back the loan, over many months, with interest, on time, every month.

When the lender reviews the loan application, it should be obvious that lending money to you, for your business, is a great way for the lending institution to make money.

You'll have to demonstrate to the lender that you:

1. Thoroughly understand the business you're starting

2. Have a history of being a good credit risk

3. Have a plan that makes sense compared to other similar businesses

4. Can execute the business plan and adapt to difficult situations

Businesses typically write a business plan that they can give to lenders and investors to show how the business will be started and operated. Your knowledge of financial statements and how your business will make money will also be a major part of building the plan.

The business plan is a standard part of any business loan application process. It should make a convincing case that the lender should lend you the money because it will be profitable for the lender to do so.

Demonstrate an Understanding

If you're asking a lender to lend money to your business, it's very important that you're able to demonstrate that you thoroughly understand the business.

The lender will want to know about your prior experience in the same type of business. It will be very comforting for the lender to know that you have experience and a demonstrated record of success in the same type of business, or that you'll be able to transfer skills from another field in the operation of this company. The lender will also look to you to provide an overview of how the industry functions and how your business will operate within that industry. In addition, the lender will want to know who your major competitors are and how you intend to compete against them.

It's very important that you're able to not only discuss the strategy your business will use to gain a competitive advantage but that you can explain the typical margins and other ratios for the industry and your business. You should also be ready to explain any differences between your business and what's typical for the industry.

If you don't understand, or are not able to explain, all the ins and outs of running the business, it's very unlikely that the lender will be willing to take a risk and lend you any money. The key questions a lender might ask in an effort to gain an understanding of the business and your knowledge of it are listed in "Business Knowledge Checklist" on page 294. You should have addressed these questions in your business plan and be prepared to answer them when meeting with the lender.

BUSINESS KNOWLEDGE CHECKLIST

❑ How long have you worked in the same business?

❑ Was that business successful? How so? If it wasn't successful, why not?

❑ Did you run the business or were you a subordinate? Explain your role.

❑ Do you know the business from an owner's standpoint? How so?

❑ How long did you work there? Why did you leave?

❑ What are the business's most profitable products or services?

❑ What products or services are unprofitable?

❑ Why are unprofitable products offered by businesses in this field?

❑ What are the primary financial indicators of success or problems in the business?

❑ What are the performance ratios that indicate success or problems?

❑ What's a good figure? What's a bad figure?

❑ Who is your competition in the field?

❑ Who will be the toughest competitor? Why?

❑ What's the failure rate of similar businesses in this community?

❑ Have you ever failed in business? Why? What did you learn from the experience?

Demonstrate Strong Credit

To obtain a loan, it's very important that the lender consider you and the business to be a good credit risk. In addition to using your credit score, the lender may evaluate your credit worthiness the old-fashioned way—by asking you about your credit history, listening to your answers, and trying to gain an understanding of your attitude toward paying your debts.

The lender wants to make sure that you—and your business—regard the payment of your debts as a financial obligation and that you'll work diligently to make sure the required payments are made.

When lenders make a loan, they expect to be paid back. If the lender sees through your credit history that you have a record of not making your payments, or determines as a result of the interview that you don't feel an obligation to pay your debts, you won't get a loan. Be prepared: The "Credit History Checklist" below contains a list of questions the lender might ask about your credit history in an effort to decide if you and your business are a good credit risk.

CREDIT HISTORY CHECKLIST

- ❑ Have you ever had credit? Why? Tell me about the loans you have now.
- ❑ How have you handled the credit you've had? Explain.
- ❑ What's your credit score? Why is it so low or high? (You must know your credit score)
- ❑ Have you ever gone bankrupt? Why?
- ❑ Have you ever defaulted on a loan? Why?
- ❑ Have you ever been late on a loan payment? Why? Be prepared to discuss any late payment or loan charge off on your credit report.
- ❑ Have you or anyone with whom you file taxes jointly ever had a tax lien? Why?
- ❑ Have you ever worked in a business that went belly up? Why did that happen?
- ❑ Have you ever co-signed on a loan? Why? Tell me about the experience.
- ❑ Have you ever been a co-borrower on a loan? Why? Tell me about the experience.
- ❑ Have you ever lent money to anyone? Why? Tell me about the experience.
- ❑ Show me your last three years of tax returns. Tell me about them.

Present a Plan

A lender will also want to review your plan for starting and operating the business. First, the lender wants to know that you have a plan. This indicates that you've given the creation and operation of the business some thought. Hopefully, a great deal of thought. You'll need to convince the lender that the plan for the business makes sense.

If you have a written business plan, the lender will want to make certain that you understand its contents and that all of the parts fit together. This is particularly important if you didn't write the business plan yourself but hired someone else to write it. Even if you hired someone else to write your plan, it's your plan, and you'll need to demonstrate that you understand its contents.

The financial statements and financial projections section of the plan will be very important to the lender. The lender will be looking to see that everything makes sense and that the business is making, or will make, enough money to be able to pay back the loan. For a list of some questions the lender may ask about the business plan and financial projections, see the checklist below.

BUSINESS PLAN AND FINANCIAL PROJECTIONS CHECKLIST

- ❏ Do you have a business plan? Why or why not?
- ❏ Did you put the plan together, or did someone else?
- ❏ Is this the first time you've written a business plan?
- ❏ Does the plan have three years of projections for the cash flow, profit and loss and balance sheet? Walk me through those financial statements.
- ❏ Do the financial statements sum and calculate correctly? (*Don't laugh; this can be a deal killer if the lender checks and finds any error.*)
- ❏ Show me the critical ratios for the business, and tell me what the typical figures are in this business field.

Execute the Plan

Finally, you must be able to convince the lender that you can execute the business plan. The lender will want to know about the qualifications of any other staff the business has or plans to hire. The lender will also want to know about any functions, such as accounting or payroll, that you plan to outsource. If you don't have expertise in a particular area, the lender will be looking to see if that knowledge is available from the staff or outside professionals you plan to hire.

Most important, the lender will want to know about the cash the business has available to meet its operating needs and any unexpected expenses. The lender will want to make sure there's additional cash available to the business should operations not go as planned.

You'll need to convince the lender that you can execute the business plan and adapt to difficult situations, should they arise. Make sure you're ready to answer any questions the lender might ask about the execution of the business plan by studying the list on page 298.

BUSINESS OPERATIONS CHECKLIST

❑ Walk me through the business plan.

❑ Do you have the bookkeeping staff and accounting software necessary to track your business results? Can you use the software, or will you depend on someone else?

❑ Have you adequately planned for the cash you'll need? How do you know?

❑ Have you projected your financial statements through multiple what-if scenarios? Tell me about the situations that would be a problem for the business and how you would address those problems.

❑ Will you sign personal guarantees for the loans? Why or why not?

❑ Will you provide collateral for the loan in the form of a mortgage on your home? Why or why not?

❑ What other sources of emergency funds do you have? What could you sell to raise cash?

Outside Investors and Venture Capitalists

There may be times when you need to look beyond your money, your family and friends, and a bank loan as a source of funds to start or grow your business. This might occur when your business is growing, but you (and your family and friends) have already invested quite a bit of money in the business. It might also occur when you've created a business with lots of growth potential, but it isn't generating enough cash flow to be able to make payments on a loan.

When this happens, you might approach our final source of startup capital: an outside investor or venture capitalist to invest in your business. An outside investor is any unrelated person or organization that invests in your business. Outside investors can include wealthy individuals in your community who invest in new ventures as a sideline, or they can be professionals who make a living investing in businesses for themselves or on behalf of their clients, or anywhere in between.

When outside INVESTORS or VENTURE CAPITALISTS invest in your business, they receive an OWNERSHIP INTEREST in the business.

Venture capitalists are a special type of outside investor who specialize in providing startup and growth financing to businesses with exceptional growth potential. Venture capitalists are very common in the computer and software industry as well as in certain parts of the pharmaceutical and medical fields.

Obtaining startup capital from outside investors and venture capitalists is not only very difficult, but you'll find that these types of investors aren't as warm and cuddly as lenders from banks, credit unions or community loan funds.

Outside investors and venture capitalists invest in businesses with the expectation of making a return on their investment for themselves and their clients. Typically, an investment from an outside investor or venture capitalist in a business is made in the form of an equity investment rather than a loan. When outside investors or venture capitalists invest in your business, they receive an ownership interest in the business. That is, they own a piece of your business. Depending on the amount of money they provide and the terms you negotiate, they may own a small percentage of the business or a large percentage.

Plus, everything you'll need to do for banks and credit unions you'll need to do for these investors as well, only more so. Professional equity investors and venture capitalists will review the strategy of the business and look to understand why this will give the business a competitive advantage. They'll also look at the operating strategy and at how the business will make money. While a lender will often look through your business plan for this information, an outside investor will not only look at the business plan but will also meet with you to assess your understanding of the business and your ability to carry out the business plan.

Quite often, outside investors and venture capitalists are investing as much in the individuals who run the business as they are in the business plan. Before outside investors or venture capitalists will invest in your business, they need to make certain that you and your management team have the willingness and ability to run the operation. If they don't feel a connection to you or feel you're the right person to run the business, they won't invest.

Many an investor has TURNED AWAY an investment opportunity when the financial projections presented in the business plan DIDN'T MAKE SENSE.

Finally, outside investors and venture capitalists will want to make sure the business has the means to repay their investment. These types of investors often expect returns on their investments of 20 percent or more. If the business can't offer returns this high, they most likely won't invest.

You can expect outside investors and venture capitalists to spend considerable time evaluating the financial projections of the business. Essentially, they'll be reviewing your financial projections to make sure that they make sense. The financial statements should tie together. The profitability, efficiency, liquidity and leverage ratios should be consistent with the industry, and if not, you should be able to explain why they're different.

You should know the numbers that are in your financial projections and you should present your financial projections in a manner that's clear and concise. To help you with these projections, one excellent source of information is the forecasting and projection spreadsheets that are available on our website (www.FinanceWithoutFear.com) as well as the forecasting and projections chapters in the companion workbook *Finance Without Fear Business Forecasting Workbook.*

If you've used what you've learned from the ratio and analysis chapters of this book, you should have a good idea whether your projections make sense, and you can use some of the available ratio information to justify your projections.

If the investors see that you've done your homework and understand the financial aspects of the business, they'll be much more likely to invest. Many an investor has turned away an investment opportunity when the financial projections presented in the business plan didn't make sense.

As you can see, obtaining funding from outside investors and venture capitalists can be a complex and expensive process. Many businesses leave this source of capital as a last resort, until the business has a significant success record, and they can get favorable terms from these investors. But if your business needs money to grow and has the potential to generate attractive profits, outside investors and venture capitalists can be an excellent source of financing.

About the Authors

WILLIAM S. HETTINGER, PH.D., is an internationally known consultant and educator with more than 20 years' experience in finance, real estate, and innovation and entrepreneurship. As an educator, he has trained numerous students in entrepreneurship and small-business creation. His consulting practice focuses on helping organizations and individuals turn ideas into actions. His client base includes small businesses, Fortune 500 companies, nonprofits, and community organizations.

Dr. Hettinger earned his Ph.D. in international development from the University of Southern Mississippi, an MBA from Rensselaer Polytechnic Institute, and a bachelor's degree from the University of Buffalo. He is the author of the book *Living and Working in Paradise: Why Housing Is Too Expensive and What Communities Can Do About It* (Thames River Publishing).

JOHN DOLAN-HEITLINGER is a nationally known consultant and business executive with more than 20 years' experience as a CEO and senior executive in financial institutions. His national consulting practice assists financial institutions and small businesses with governance, planning, financial management, mergers, and regulatory issues. He has chaired and served on many civic, not-for-profit, and government boards.

Mr. Dolan-Heitlinger earned his MBA from the Johnson School at Cornell University and a bachelor's degree in history and economics from SUNY Potsdam. He is a nationally recognized speaker and regular contributor to professional journals. He is retired from the U.S. Coast Guard Reserve as a Commander.

Index